D0409342

FOSTER'S EVEN ODDER IRISH ODDITIES

Allen Foster was born in Dublin in 1974 and works as a researcher and a writer. He previously wrote a biography of the eccentric American George Francis Train, inspiration for Jules Vernes's classic fictional hero Phileas Fogg, as well as the bestselling *Foster's Irish Oddities*. He currently lives on a dairy farm in County Meath and shares fleas with a small dog called Ziggy.

FOSTER'S
EVEN ODDER
IRISH ODDITIES

A Miscellany of Strange Facts

ALLEN FOSTER

NEW
ISLAND

Foster's Even Odder Irish Oddities
First published 2007
by New Island
2 Brookside
Dundrum Road
Dublin 14
www.newisland.ie

© Allen Foster 2007

The author has asserted his moral rights.

ISBN 978-1-905494-76-7

All rights reserved. The material in this publication is protected by copyright law. Except as may be permitted by law, no part of the material may be reproduced (including by storage in a retrieval system) or transmitted in any form or by any means; adapted; rented or lent without the written permission of the copyright owners.

British Library Cataloguing in Publication Data. A CIP catalogue record for this book is available from the British Library.

Illustrations by Dougie Ferris
Printed in Finland by WS Bookwell

10 9 8 7 6 5 4 3 2 1

SOUTH EASTERN EDUCATION AND LIBRARY BOARD	
0758247	
RONDO	10/12/2007
941.5	£ 9.99
SELOCAL	

INTRODUCTION

Foster's Even Odder Irish Oddities is a collection of strange Irish trivia. This book and its companion volume, *Foster's Irish Oddities*, are essentially Irish versions of the wonderful *Ripley's Believe It or Not* books that were once extremely popular. Robert Ripley travelled the world looking for strange facts. I made do looking through old books, newspapers and archives in Dublin libraries.

If you like this book, you will love the *Fortean Times* (www.forteantimes.com), a monthly magazine dedicated to the strange and unusual.

Painstaking efforts have been made to ensure that all the bizarre trivia within *Foster's Even Odder Irish Oddities* are correct. In a book with so many facts, it would be hard to believe that some errors have not been made. If you spot any mistakes or would like to contribute any strange facts, please email them to Irishfacts@eircom.net or send them to the author, c/o New Island, 2 Brookside, Dundrum Road, Dundrum, Dublin 14.

Many people deserve mention for their part in this book's creation. Chief amongst them are Jonathan Williams, the good people of New Island, Michael Potterton, William Montgomery, Denis Curtin, Raymond Coyle, Margaret McAuliffe of Cobh Museum, Frank Pelly of the Irish Lighthouse Museum (www.cil.ie), Robert Campbell-Lloyd of www.kitecompany.com, Paul Sieveking and Dougie Ferris, for his excellent illustrations. Mandy and Leo Dickinson of www.adventurearchive.com were an excellent source of information about Noel Farrelly.

Allen Foster
October 2007

To my mother and father

WILLIAM Clark (1677–1738) from Newmarket, County Cork is Ireland's most famous 'ossified man', not least because his skeleton is on display in the Anatomy Museum of Trinity College, Dublin. He suffered from a rare affliction which got worse as he grew old. Essentially his muscles turned to bone and his joints fused together. In his infancy, it had been noted that he never turned his head or bent his body. In his youth, he could never put his hands behind his back or lift them higher than the level of his elbow. In adulthood, his jaws became one solid mass and he had to be fed liquid food through a hole made in his front teeth. When his body was dissected after his death, it was found to be one solid mass of bone from the top of his head to his knees. The unfortunate man must have suffered terribly. A reasonable account of Clark features in Charles Smith's *History of Cork*.

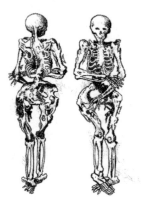

A BONY substance grew out of William Clark's left heel and usually reached about two inches before it dropped off. Philip Luckombe, who published *A Tour through Ireland* in 1783, says, 'Among other things, I was shown here [in Cork City] a set of knives and forks, whose handles were made out of the heels of the wonderful ossified body of the man I saw in Trinity College, Dublin; he was a native of this place. These bones grew in the form of a cock's-spur [*sic*], but much larger, as you may imagine, since the handles are of a common size. These were not sawed off, but fell yearly, like the horns of a stag, without any pain to the limbs that bore them. They were well polished, and of a very hard substance, equal to ivory, though not so white.'

∽

A LESS well-known ossified man is mentioned in the *Annual Register* of 1759. Nineteen-year-old William Carey from near Lough Melvin, County Leitrim attracted the attentions of learned gentlemen and doctors. The Reverend William Henry of Castle Caldwell, near Enniskillen, County Fermanagh extensively documented the youth's case. Carey was in perfect health until August 1757, when he first felt an unusual pain in his right wrist. It was so bad that he had to give up his job as a labourer. Over the next few months his arm swelled and his muscles turned into a substance like bone. The same thing happened with his left arm and, later in March 1758, to his right ankle and subsequently continued spreading upwards towards his knee.

The Reverend Henry sent Carey to Mercers Hospital in Dublin. Doctors there applied mercury-based plasters to his body. This seemed to help the teenager, but did not reverse the ossification of his body. In any case, he could now move his elbows and fingers more easily. Carey was discharged from the hospital with instructions to keep applying the plasters to his ossified parts. They also told him to bathe regularly in the ocean (which he lived close to) and to take seaweed baths. His ultimate fate does not seem to have been recorded.

∽

IN early April 1977, 35-year-old Dublin man Noel Farrelly fell 7,000 feet and survived after his main parachute failed and his reserve opened only partially. The incident occurred at Shobdon Airfield, Hereford, in England, where Farrelly was practising with the rest of his parachuting team for the Irish championships. His life was saved by a well-placed tree, which broke his fall. Noel survived, but was hospitalised with multiple injuries. Inside two years he was back parachuting. Filmmakers Mandy and Leo Dickinson included an excellent re-enactment of the incident, along with an interview with Noel Farrelly, in their stunning documentary *Dead Men's Tales*.

∽

JOSEPH Allen, a well-known auctioneer from Cookstown, County Tyrone, had a lucky escape from death on the night of 10 January 1932. He owed his life to a gold watch, which was in his pocket. He was leaving his office after closing up for the night when two raiders ordered him to put up his hands. Two shots were fired, the second bullet striking the watch, piercing it and inflicting a slight wound on Allen's abdomen. The men got away, but Allen identified one of them and he was caught. Allen had a large sum of money on his person at the time, but the raiders did not get it.

∽

A DUEL was fought in Marylebone Fields, London by two Irish hairdressers on 22 October 1766. Their seconds were two journeymen tailors, who, unbeknownst to the hairdressers, had loaded both pistols with half-boiled potatoes.

∽

AN extraordinary freak of nature was discovered at the Cappoquin Bacon Factory, County Waterford in early June 1936. After slaughtering a batch of fat pigs, staff discovered that one of the animals had two hearts. They were on the same side of its body. In all other respects the pig appeared perfectly normal. The veterinary surgeon supervising the killings, Robert Byrne, from Dungarvan, considered this anomaly to be so unusual that he sent the two hearts to a museum in Dublin to be preserved.

∽

ON 14 June 1794, a young Carlingford (County Louth) woman's fatal curiosity about the contents of a cask hidden in a garden near where she lived had terrible consequences. She stuck a heated poker into the cask. Unfortunately, it was full of gunpowder and the girl was blown to pieces. Small pieces of her body were found at great distances from the scene of the accident. Four houses were also destroyed as a result of the foolish girl's idle snooping and the explosion smashed most of the town's windows.

∽

IN 1819, Thomas Hall, an ingenious Irish linen weaver, manufactured a complete shirt entirely on his loom. It was woven throughout without seams, and accurately and neatly gathered at the neck, shoulders and wrists. The neck and wristbands were doubled and stitched; there was a regular selvage on each side of the breast, and the shoulder straps and gussets were neatly stitched, as well as the wrists. In short, it was as perfectly finished, as if made by an expert seamstress. The shirt was exhibited and several people involved in the linen trade were perfectly satisfied that it had been made entirely on a loom without any assistance from a needle.

∽

BERNARD Lynch, the captain of Woodbrook golf club near Bray, County Wicklow, holed in one on 7 April 1945. Later the same day another player holed in one on the same course. His name was also Bernard Lynch – but they were not related.

∽

THE town books of the Corporation of Youghal, County Cork are full of many curiosities. In the years 1680 and 1700 respectively, a cook and a barber were made freemen, on condition that they should severally dress the mayor's feasts and shave the Corporation free of charge. On 29 September 1610 the town council was so concerned about 'divers lewd and incontinent persons' deflowering virgins that they passed a law against them. The offender was faced with a choice of paying a fine to or marrying the young girl. There was a sliding scale of amounts payable according to the girl's station, and they were as follows: £40 for a mayor's daughter, £30 for an alderman's daughter, £20 for a bailiff's daughter, £10 for any freeman's daughter and £5 for a groom's daughter.

‿

FROM the *Annals of the Four Masters*:
1488. A wonderful child was born in Dublin, who had his teeth at his birth; he grew to an enormous size, and so large a person was not heard of since the time of the heroes.

1489. The sheep of that part of Meath verging on the sea from Dublin to Drogheda ran into the sea in despite of their shepherds, and never returned.

‿

IN July 1954 Siamese twin roses were discovered growing on a bush in the garden of Dr E.M. Finegan of Carlingford, County Louth. Both flowers were perfectly formed and had a common stem and calyx, the sepals of which were the correct number for a single rose bloom. Gardening experts said that it was highly unusual. The rose was called Golden Dawn.

‿

'I RECOLLECT,' says the celebrated writer Jonah Barrington (1760–1834), 'in the Queen's County [present-day County Laois], to have seen a Mr Clerk, who had been a working carpenter, and when making a bench for the session justices at the Court-house, was laughed at for taking peculiar pains in planning and smoothing the seat of it. He smilingly observed, "that he did so to *make it easy for himself*, as he was resolved he would never die till he had a right to sit thereupon," and he kept his word. He was an industrious man – honest, respectable and kind-hearted. He succeeded in all his efforts to accumulate an independence – he did accumulate it, and uprightly. His character kept pace with the increase of his property, and he lived to sit, as a magistrate, on that very bench that he sawed and planed.'

❧

BECAUSE he wanted an Irish family living near him to have a 'little bit of Ireland' in their home, Londoner David Delvin of Woodward Road, Dulwich ordered one ton of turf to be delivered to Patrick Murphy of Underhill Road, Dulwich in early October 1960. Originally the turf cost a little over £5, but as a result of freight, customs clearance and local delivery charges, the cost went up to nearly £20. Mr Delvin said, 'It's worth it for the happiness it will bring to a wonderful family who have been so long away from Ireland.'

❧

THE world's smallest kites were invented by the Campbell-Lloyd family of Branchfield House, Ballymote, County Sligo. What originally started as a home schooling project on the family's kitchen table in 1995 is now a thriving business and the kites are sold worldwide. The tiny kites are so small, they fit in the palm of your hand and come in a wide range of shapes and colours, from flying pigs to shamrocks.

❧

IN December 1993, 35-year-old Belfast man Danny Harper regained his sight for the first time in 16 years when he was hit on the head by a falling chicken carcass. Moira Dunleavy had dropped the chicken from the tenth floor of her tower block. 'It smelled a bit off,' she explained.

꿍

VETERAN Dublin-born BBC television reporter Peter Snow was lucky to survive after a light plane in which he was a passenger crashed into trees on Bainbridge Island, off Seattle, in early October 1999. This island happened to be the setting of a best-selling novel, *Snow Falling on Cedars*, by David Guterson.

꿍

JOHN Langley, an Englishman who settled in Ireland, where he died, left the following extraordinary will: 'I, John Langley, born at Wincanton in Somersetshire and settled in Ireland in the year 1651, now in my right mind and wits, do make my will in my own hand-writing. I do leave all my house, goods, and farm of Black Kettle of 253 acres to my son, commonly called Stubborn Jack, to him and heirs forever, provided he marries a Protestant, but not Alice Kendrick, who called me "Oliver's whelp". My new buck-skin breeches and my silver tobacco stopper with J.L. on the top, I give to Richard Richards, my comrade, who helped me off at the storming of Clonmell when I was shot through the leg. My said son John shall keep my body above ground six days and six nights after I am dead; and Grace Kendrick shall lay me out, who shall have for so doing Five Shillings. My body shall be put upon the oak table in the brown room, and 50 Irish men shall be invited to my wake, and every one shall have two quarts of the best Acqua vitae, and each one skein [a small knife], dish, and knife before him: and when the liquor is out, nail up my coffin and commit me to the earth whence I came. This is my will, witness my hand this 3rd of March, 1674. John Langley.'

Before his death, some of Langley's friends asked him why he had gone to the expense of treating Irishmen so well since he hated them. He replied that if they got drunk at his wake, they would probably start fighting and kill one another, which would do something towards lessening the breed!

~

THE Proctor's accounts of Christ Church, Dublin contain many entries in which the names of Thomas Flood and John Wolfe figure. These two gentlemen were the vergers, bell-ringers and general handymen of the cathedral from 1680 to 1690. From what can be gathered, their activities sometimes extended to other directions by no means pleasing to the civic authorities. In 1684 they led a mob which successfully resisted the Sheriff of Dublin's attempts to arrest a fugitive within the 'Liberties' of the cathedral, but were later seized by a force of '40 constables' and 'dragged by the hair of their heads to gaole'.

Subsequent imprisonments for similar offences are faithfully recorded, including one for the possession of concealed weapons, which necessitated a petition from the Dean and Chapter to King James II. The most curious charge of all for which Flood and Wolfe suffered was brought against them in 1688, when the Lord Mayor had them clapped into the stocks because he 'fancied they did not make the bells ring merrily enough for the birth of the Prince of Wales'.

❧

IN March 1933 a five-legged lamb was born on a farm near St Kearn's, County Wexford.

❧

BALLINROBE-born John King hitchhiked his way to greatness when he left Mayo in 1893 with £70 in his pocket and arrived in New York with £2 10s. Twice he won the highest award for heroism in America – the Congressional Medal – while serving in the US Navy. Although he died in 1938, the navy remembered his heroism by naming a missile-destroyer the *USS John King* in 1960.

❧

JOHN Kelly from Rhode, County Offaly owned a donkey that brought him £25,000 in 1960. Here's how it came about: John sold the donkey to tinkers and with the proceeds bought a ticket in the Hospitals' Sweepstakes. The ticket drew Fougable, on which all the villagers (with the exception of John) had a flutter. Meanwhile, John's donkey became homesick for his old home and wandered away from his new owners. On the morning of the race, the donkey walked into John's kitchen. 'It's good luck,' was John's comment, and so the donkey stayed. After winning the money, John was anxious to keep the donkey and told newspapers that he would like to find the tinkers to pay them back – even if they raised the price.

❧

THE Dublin Medical Press of 1855 contains an account of the removal of an inch-long horn from the lower lip of a 70-year-old Dublin man. It was more than an inch and a half in circumference at its widest part. The horn was shaped like an animal's claw, being slightly curved, narrow and pointed at its tip. It was located just a little to the left of the centre of his lips and had been there for several years, but before the operation it had started to grow. At the time of its removal there was hardly any bleeding, but a few hours later the wound started to haemorrhage badly. With great difficulty the flow was stemmed and the man lived for some time afterwards.

∽

TWO butchers (brothers) had a dispute on the morning of 20 October 1765 in Clarendon Market, Dublin. One of them stabbed the other with a knife twice in the stomach. He was carried to the infirmary while his brother was lodged in Newgate Prison.

∽

EXTRACT of a letter from a gentleman at Ovens, County Cork, dated 1 October 1765:

'Last Saturday morning about eight o'clock as I walked out, near 200 yards from the house, I perceived an abundance of glutinous matter, lying on the grass and hedges, strongly resembling fresh butter, in substance, taste, and colour; which, as I cannot otherwise account for it, must in my opinion, have fallen on the earth as a shower. Being anxious to discover its real substance or to know in what time it would dissolve, I collected and brought home a considerable quantity. But the sample I now send, ye will see how nearly it preserves a likeness to the description as when fresh. The mentioning of this fact, I think, is worthy a place in your paper, as it may probably attract the attention of the curious.'

∽

TOWARDS the end of September 1765, 25-year-old James Burns of Monasterevin, County Kildare married a 95-year-old widow called Glover of Strand Street. He was her fifth husband.

∽

THE oldest woman in Northern Ireland, 103-year-old Mary Sweeney of Hollywood, County Down, had her first ride in a helicopter on 17 May 1978. 'It was lovely,' she quipped. 'I might do it again.' In preparation for her afternoon flight, Mary had a light lunch, and before getting into the helicopter had a smoke from one of her favourite clay pipes. The helicopter, piloted by Major Colm Sibun, whisked Mary across the rooftops of some of her friends' houses in Belfast. Afterwards Major Sibun told reporters, 'She was very relaxed and waved down to the people. She seemed to enjoy it.' Mary lived at Edgecombe House, an old people's home on the outskirts of Belfast. Every day she got up at 6:30 and helped to prepare breakfast, and later lunch and the evening meal. It had been her ambition for a couple of years to fly in a helicopter. Her wish was made known to Belfast City Council's Leisure Centre's department and they arranged for her outing.

∽

THE Freeman's Journal of 12 September 1795 contains the following observation about Dublin night watchmen: 'The new watch for St Andrew's parish are to be equipped with a helmet, a pole, a bayonet, a lantern, and a clapper to give alarm. The bayonet is contrived to fit upon the end of the pole, to which it is only affixed in case of necessity. Other parishes have adopted a pole with a hook and spear to it, and some a pole with a hanger; but the accoutrement intended for St Andrew's watch appears to be best calculated for service.'

∾

IRISHWOMAN Hannah Dagoe was sentenced to death at the Old Bailey, London for robbing another poor woman of all her belongings. She was hanged at Tyburn, London on 4 May 1763, but she went out in style and in a way of her own choosing, rather than suffer a slow, painful death while 'dancing' on the gallows. When the cart in which she was bound reached the gallows, she freed her arms loose and attacked her executioner, Thomas Turlis, daring him to hang her. She punched him so violently that she almost knocked him down.

She then threw her hat, cloak and several other items of clothing into the crowd in order to cheat Turlis of the hangman's traditional right to dispose (for profit) of the possessions of the condemned. Eventually Dagoe was overpowered and the hangman got the rope around her neck. But before the signal could be given for the cart to move off and the condemned woman to be hanged by slow strangulation, Dagoe bound a handkerchief around her head and over her face and threw herself out of the cart with such violence that she broke her neck and died instantly.

❧

IN a number of the *Dublin Journal of Medical and Chemical Sciences*, Professor Robert Graves (1796–1853) published an account of a 47-year-old woman who had fractured a rib during a violent fit of coughing. She felt a stitch in her left side, accompanied by a sensation of something having snapped or given way.

❧

THE practice of selling provisions from barrows and stalls set along city pavements is undoubtedly an ancient one. It is probably one of the earliest methods of trading. In the 17th century, every trader (usually a woman) in the streets of Dublin selling her goods at a stall, or from a basket or barrow, was charged a toll of one farthing per week, to be used to fund the cleansing of the street as well as the stalls. It seems that there was no public expenditure on keeping the city's streets clean; this appears to have been the responsibility of the citizens themselves. Each householder was obliged to pay for the cleaning and paving of that portion of the street immediately in front of their dwelling.

One woman, the aptly named Katherine Strong, inherited the lucrative office of Dublin City Scavenger from her husband and became notorious as a toll-collector. She paid more attention to collecting tolls than to keeping the streets clean and was unduly hard on street traders. During the bitterly harsh winter of 1635, it is recorded that a huge snow effigy of the unpopular widow was erected in one of

the city's main streets. The snow woman was superbly detailed, even down to holding a representation of the hated
toll in one hand. What the grasping widow made of it is
not recorded.

꿍

DERRY solicitor Kevin Agnew's life was saved by a
timely lunch break on 4 May 1978. While Agnew was
eating a meal in his Maghera home, his car was blown up
by a 4 lb bomb. Earlier, Agnew, a well-known member of
Sinn Féin, had driven nine miles to Magherafelt Court and
home again – not knowing that he was sitting just above a
bomb. Police believed the bomb had been fitted to the car
the previous night.

꿍

FEW people realise that the six of hearts is nicknamed
Grace's Card after a defiant Irish soldier. Richard Grace,
who was subsequently killed at the Battle of Athlone in
1691, was invited to join the Williamite forces, and wrote
his reply, rejecting the proposal, on the back of a six of
hearts.

꿍

THE *Man of Feeling*, by Edinburgh writer Henry Mackenzie, was published anonymously in 1771 and sold very well.
Bizarrely, a young Irish clergyman named Eccles tried to
claim the novel as his own work, and even went so far as
to back his claim with a manuscript in his own handwrit-
ing, complete with deletions, corrections and changes.
MacKenzie and his publisher denounced this fraudulent
claim and proved the novel's provenance. When Eccles

died, his tombstone repeated his false claims. Mackenzie was a prolific and versatile writer, but none of his works attained the success or controversy of *The Man of Feeling*.

❧

IN 1931, a very apt memorial to the inventor of the pneumatic tyre, J.B. Dunlop, was unveiled in Belfast. What was so apt about the statue? It was made entirely of rubber – the same material that made his invention a possibility! It was shaped from a block of hard rubber weighing about 270 pounds, subjected to a pressure of 250 tons and then baked for 110 hours. The result was a material that, it was hoped, would be 'more enduring than brass'. Another curious feature of this memorial is that after the portrait had been copied upon the rubber from the sculptor's clay model, the lettering 'was done by a burr with six microscopic cutting edges, such as is used by dentists in preparing teeth for filling'.

❧

A BULL broke loose in the Shankill Road district of Belfast in early August 1927 and ran amok through the principal streets of the city. One of its pursuers secured a motor car, from which the animal was cleverly lassoed after a two-mile chase to the outskirts of the city. The bull was then tethered to a tramway standard and subsequently removed in a van.

❧

IRISHWOMAN Mrs Laetitia Sage became the first woman in England to take to the air. Towards the end of May 1795 she made her ascent in Lunardi's balloon from the obelisk in St George's Fields, London. This adventure was a success, capturing the public's imagination and making Mrs Sage famous. Shortly afterwards she and the balloon went on display at the Pantheon in Paris, where she proudly answered questions about her aerial trip. A supper and dance were held in her honour. Mrs Sage seems to have had a flair for self-publicity, for she continued to profit from her balloon flight for a long time afterwards. When the novelty of her undertaking wore off, she managed to acquire a bruised foot and regained the limelight. The public willingly paid 5 shillings to see her, and prints of her by the famous Italian engraver Bartolozzi sold widely.

∽

ON New Year's Eve 1929, Michael J. Kavanagh, a solicitor in Wexford, shot three geese on the south Wexford sloblands with one shot, using an ordinary 12-bore gun. All three birds fell quite close to one other, two stone dead and the third mortally wounded.

∽

THE retirement of a remarkable Waterford man was announced in many Irish newspapers in early March 1933. Seventy-five-year-old Johnny Power of Kilcanavee, Kilmacthomas was known all over Munster. He travelled many thousands of miles during his lifetime, but he never walked. He spent thousands of pounds purchasing eggs in different parts of the country, yet he never handled an egg or penny, because he was both legless and armless.

Unlike Arthur MacMurrogh Kavanagh (1831–89) of County Carlow, who was also born with the same physical defects, but was from a wealthy background, John Power had only his own determination to help him triumph over his disabilities. He became an egg dealer in his youth and overcame his handicap in an ingenious way.

He bought a pony and cart and specially trained the animal to convey him through the countryside – even through the thickest city traffic – without reins or guidance beyond his spoken word. Johnny talked to his pony, and the animal understood every direction he gave. They never had an accident. When purchasing quantities of eggs, Johnny simply told the vendor what he would offer for them, and, if a deal followed, the money was removed from a bag which he carried in the cart. He never lost a penny and never had too much or too little taken from him.

◆

ANOTHER remarkable limbless Waterford person was Johanna Megrines, who was born in Dungarvan on 5 January 1702. According to James Paris du Plessis in his unpublished manuscript, *History of Prodigies*, she 'was very thin. Her father carried her upon his back a-begging, till she growing so big and fat, and her father so old and feeble, could carry her no longer, so she was forced to drag herself upon a leather cushion fastened to her. She could dance, skip and lift, very nimbly. She could take up from the ground any piece of money, be it ever so small, also pins, needles and nails, with her stumps.'

◆

HUGH Robinson survived a 110,000-volt electric shock after a ladder he was carrying touched an overhead cable at the new Derry city power station on 29 January 1962. The 29-year-old would have been killed instantly if he had not been wearing rubber boots and carrying a wooden ladder. The rubber boots melted on his legs.

❧

AN ankle competition at a fancy dress carnival in Newry, County Down in November 1927 resulted in an easy win for a mere man over 20 female competitors. Constable R.S.J. Fowlie, who was attached to Canal Street Barracks, attended the carnival dressed as 'Miss 1927' and he entered for the contest. The competitors were placed behind a screen. Unaware of the identity of the possessor of the neatest ankles, the judges made their award, the result causing great hilarity.

❧

A FROG called 'Mighty Toor Lock' made a leap of 14 feet 3 inches on 20 May 1956 to win third place for Ireland at the world championships of the International Frog Jumping Olympics in Angel Falls, California. Owned by Frank McNeff, a native of Turlough, County Mayo, then living in California, the frog was flown in from Ireland and given a two-day course before entering the contest. 'Buck Junior', a long-legged American entrant, beat 200 frogs from Germany, Italy, France, Japan, Australia and Canada and received first prize. His leap, watched by 22,000 people, was 15 feet 9 inches. Japan's entry was not in leaping form at all, and jumped only 2 feet 5.5 inches.

❧

THE *Dublin Medical Journal* of 1837 contains a report of a brewery man who had fallen under his heavily laden dray. It crossed his chest. When he was picked up off the road, he complained of pain and weakness, but continued to drive the dray for another hour. As he neared a hospital, he thought he might as well get himself examined. He walked in and lay on a bed. He turned on one side and suddenly expired. An autopsy discovered that a wound in the heart had been plugged by a fractured rib. When he had turned on his side, the rib had moved and he had haemorrhaged to death.

∽

IN 1705, a pamphlet was published in Dublin called 'The Report of the Commissioners appointed to inquire into the Irish Forfeitures', which contained matter highly offensive to the government. After it was discovered that Francis Annesley, an MP for the borough of Downpatrick, was one of the authors of the report, he was expelled from Parliament. Three other authors of the report were later discovered: James Hamilton, John Frenchard and Henry Langford. On hearing that Hamilton was dead, Parliament prudently entered the following resolution into the record: 'The House being informed that James Hamilton, of Tullamore, is dead, the House thought fit not to put further question on him.'

∽

WHEN a fire broke out in the thatch of his cottage at Castletown, Dundalk, County Louth on 30 March 1962, it was the last of several dreadful events in a very unlucky day for 75-year-old pensioner Thomas Kindlon. In the morning he had broken an ankle in a car accident. After treatment in hospital, he insisted on going home. When he got there, he found that his cottage had been broken into and his possessions scattered. That night, passers-by noticed a fire in the thatch and carried Kindlon to safety. The fire brigade extinguished the blaze.

∾

AN amusing handbill was found stuck up in several parts of Dublin on 31 July 1784. Its text reads:

'This is to certify that I, Daniel O'Flannaghan, was not the person that was tarred and feathered by the Liberty mob on Tuesday last. And I am ready to give 20 guineas to any one that will lay me 50 that I am the other man that goes by my name.
Witness my hand this 30th of July 1784,
Daniel O'Flannaghan.'

∾

ONCE upon a time, the Dublin City Fathers regulated, or tried to regulate, not only what members of the corporate body should, or should not, wear, but the dress of every citizen. In the reign of Edward IV (1461–63), a city ordinance was passed that any citizen who used 'a mantle for his daily garment outwards', except at the town meeting, 'shall lose 6d'. Similarly, any 'woman of whatsoever condition living in Dublin was forbidden to wear a saffron smock or a saffron kerchief upon the pain of 6d'. About 150 years later, the City Fathers were concerned about the colours of their corporate robes. An order was made by them in 1608 that the younger aldermen were to wear violet gowns, the older aldermen scarlet gowns, the Sheriffs partlet gowns and the rest were to wear turkey gowns.

∽

KING James II's Irish army list shows that one Donagh O'Carroll raised a troop of cavalry consisting entirely of his 30 sons. He armed and mounted them and handed the troops over to the Earl of Ormonde in 1688. Pride must have filled his heart as he watched his troop ride off – he may have also felt a little relieved to be rid of such an unwieldy brood. Some of them, at least, he never saw again. It is said that the brothers followed the Stuarts into exile.

∽

THE first statue to a woman in the United States was erected in New Orleans in honour of Margaret Haughery (née Gaffney, 1812–82) from Tully, Carraigallen, County Leitrim. It was put up to commemorate her work for the poor of that city and her nursing services during the American Civil War.

∽

AN account of a storm which struck Athlone in 1697 and the devastating event that followed was chronicled by Governor Gustavus Hamilton in a slight pamphlet quaintly called 'A true narrative of the Prodigious Storm of Wind and Rain, Thunder and Lightening, that happened in Athlone betwixt four and five of the clock on Wednesday morning being the 27 October, 1697'.

After describing the ferocious wind, the thunder and a thick darkness that enveloped the town, Hamilton wrote, 'Broke out continued lightening, without ceasing so that

Heaven and Earth seemed to be united by ye flame, and at last fell a great body of fire directly upon the Castle, and in a moment after the Magazine took fire and blew up 250 barrels of powder, 1,000 charged hand grenades with 800 skanes of match [coils of fuse cords for gunpowder barrels], 220 barrels of musket and pistol balls, great quantities of pick-axes, spades, shovels, horse-shoes and nails, all which blew up in the air and covered ye whole town and neighbouring fields, by the volume of which the Town gates were all blown open.'

Some of the inhabitants, Hamilton says, found themselves buried in the ruins of their houses, others with their dwellings in flames. Some were blown from their beds into the street and dozens had their brains knocked out by falling stones and bursting hand grenades. In the circumstances, it is not surprising that they occupied themselves more with their prayers than with efforts to save themselves.

∽

THE nickname 'nosey parker' owes its origin to a County Laois man. Edward Parker, from Cappagh, was a sergeant in the British Army in the 19th century. Parker had a large fatty tumour right on the tip of his nose, which extended over a quarter inch below the point of his chin. In view of his affliction, soldiers of that period gave him that nickname and it stuck to him till the day of his death in 1896.

∽

ONE of the most remarkable accounts of the 'Big Wind' – the storm of January 1839 that was one of the most violent to have ever raged across Ireland – is a short letter written by the famous Irish scholar John O'Donovan, describing his experiences that night in a hotel in Glendalough, County Wicklow while sharing a room with a colleague, O'Connor. Retiring to their double-bedded room, O'Connor fell asleep quickly, but O'Donovan could not sleep. He wrote, 'At one o'clock a most tremendous hurricane commenced, which rocked the house beneath as if it were a ship. Awfully sublime, but I was much in dread that the roof would be blown off the house. I attempted to wake O'Connor by shouting to him, but could not. About two o'clock the storm became so furious that I jumped up, determined to make my way out, but I was no sooner out of bed than the window was dashed in upon the floor, and after it a squall mighty as a thunderbolt. I then, fearing that the roof would be blown off at once, pushed out the shutter and closed it as soon as the direct squall had passed off, and placed myself diagonally against it; but the next blast shot me completely out of my position and forced in the shutter. This awoke O'Connor, who was kept asleep as if by a halcyon charm. I then dressed myself, and sat at the kitchen fire till morning. Pity I have not paper to tell the rest.'

❧

A DVD spelling game hosted by presenter Eamonn Holmes had to be scrapped in October 2006 after the makers spelled his name wrongly on the cover. The Irish TV star was billed as 'Eamon Holmes' (missing the extra 'n') on the front of the interactive quiz. A furious Holmes branded the makers 'dunces'.

❧

MRS Flood of Olney, Terenure, Dublin grew a giant chrysanthemum in 1927. It was 25 feet 3 inches in circumference and was called 'Moneymaker'.

৯

FEW people realise that the upright piano was invented by a Dublin man – William Southwell. Born in 1756, Southwell was apprenticed to Weber, a celebrated harpsichord-maker of the time. In 1782, Southwell set up his own business at 26 Fleet Street and shortly afterwards took over Weber's business at 20 Marlborough Street. For many years Southwell made fine harpsichords, but changed direction at the end of 1793, when he perfected his invention of a new model pianoforte. Taking this with him, he left Dublin and opened a small shop in Lad Lane, London. The famous composer Joseph Hadyn visited and expressed so much admiration for the new instrument that Southwell took out a patent in 1794, later extending the improvements to a 'damper' action and larger compass.

Southwell's invention attracted the attention and envy of other piano-makers, notably John Broadwood, who studied his patent and was influenced by it. Southwell brought out a new model – in reality, a square piano on its side, with new action – and was granted a patent for it in 1798. This upright piano made his name and Southwell's business flourished until 1836, when he retired and returned to his native city. He died at his home in Rathmines in 1842 and is buried at Glasnevin Cemetery.

৯

JOHN Carthy, who claimed to be 116 years old, had his photograph taken for *The Irish Times* in October 1931. He lived in the same house in which he was born at Clogher, Ballinamore, County Leitrim. According to newspaper reports, he took the abstinence pledge from Father Mathew at Bawnboy, County Cavan on 1 August 1842 and remained a teetotaller ever after. He proudly displayed the pledge card he had signed at the event.

∽

A NOTE in the *Annals of the Four Masters* concerns the first camel ever seen in Ireland:

'A.D. 1472, a wonderful animal was sent to Ireland from the king of England [Edward IV]; she resembled a mare, having a yellow colour; the hoofs of a cow – a long neck, thick head, a large tail – ugly, scarce of hair. She had a peculiar saddle of her own; wheat and salt were her usual food; she used to carry the largest sled suspended from her tail: she used to kneel going under any gate, be it ever so high, and for her rider to mount.' The 'peculiar saddle' was, of course, the hump, and apparently the unfortunate animal did not escape the barbarous practice of the age, which obliged beasts of burden to pull loads by their tails.

∽

MILLIONS of flying insects invaded Lisbane district, near Killinchy, Strangford Lough, County Down, on 27 July 1956. C. Douglas Deane, curator of the Natural History Department of Belfast Museum, identified specimens that had been sent to him as a type of cranefly that had their breeding ground on Lough Neagh, about 20 miles from Lisbane. The insects were described as being about a quarter of an inch long with thin legs and wings. One resident, Mrs Evelyn Martin, vividly described the unexpected invasion: 'It was like a sudden hailstorm. We shut all the windows tightly. Any that managed to penetrate into the house we killed with DDT. Then we went outside and sprayed those on the windows. The windowsills and ground looked as if someone had emptied out pot after pot of tea-leaves.'

≈

EIGHTEEN-year-old Mary Kane from County Meath was the first Irish patient to be operated on under anaesthesia. This groundbreaking operation was performed on 1 January 1847 by Belfast-born Dr John MacDonnell. The young woman suffered from suppurative arthritis of the elbow joint following a prick of a thorn from a hawthorn branch. She had originally been scheduled to have her arm amputated just above the elbow on 31 December 1846 at Richmond Hospital, Dublin, but after reading an account of a successful operation of a patient under ether anaesthesia performed in America on 16 October 1846, Dr MacDonnell decided to postpone the operation for 24 hours. He used the extra day to construct a crude ether dispenser and tested it on himself successfully half a dozen times until he was satisfied that it would work safely. The operation was a triumph – the patient felt nothing – and heralded an important advance in medicine.

≈

FOR centuries, giant sea monsters have played a prominent part in maritime lore. On occasion, naturalists described many cases of the occurrence of giant squids and octopuses, although these accounts, until the latter part of the 19th century, were regarded as mere exaggerations. Only when specimens were observed and studied by scientists did it become accepted that all but the most exaggerated of legends of older naturalists and writers were founded on solid fact. This only shows that hidden in the depths of the oceans there may yet exist stranger creatures than any that can be dreamed of.

On 26 April 1875, a very large squid was seen and chased to the north-west of Inishbofin Island, Connemara. Fishermen in a curragh spotted a large floating mass surrounded by gulls. They pulled out to it, believing it to be a wreck, but to their astonishment found it was an enormous squid, lying perfectly still, as if basking on the surface of the water. They paddled up and cautiously lopped off one of its arms. The animal immediately set out to sea, rushing through the water at an enormous pace. The men gave chase and, after a hard pull in the frail canvas boat, caught up with it five miles out in the open Atlantic and severed another of the arms and its head. The shorter arms each measured eight feet. The tentacular arms are said to have been 30 feet long. The body sank.

෴

HARRY Houdini and other escapologists made a career of getting out of boxes, bags and restraints. Kilkenny-born Seamus Burke (1888–c.1960) became famous for getting into them. He was the world's only enterologist. After reading about a famous escapologist in a newspaper, Burke reasoned that it might be more dramatic getting into things rather than out of them.

By 1933, Burke had his unique act perfected. It consisted of three remarkable stunts. After it had been examined by the audience, Burke got into a trunk which had been encircled with rope and sealed with wax. Next he got into a sealed tissue bag handed to him after he had been heavily bound with rope. For his last trick, the Kilkenny illusionist was tied to a chair with a sealed bag draped over his shoulder. A brief while later, he was found still tied to the chair, but inside the sealed bag. Burke spent two years touring with his ingenious illusions before retiring.

∽

AMONG the curiosities of medical literature are numerous cases of patients who have contrived to harm themselves by swallowing harmful foreign bodies. Occasionally this curious pastime has had deadly consequences. One case brought before a scientific society in Dublin recorded the removal of 300 needles from a woman's body. Tragically, she died.

∽

IN November 1958 Patricia and Martin became the fourth set of twins born to Mr and Mrs Charles Courage of Ballyfermot, Dublin. The first set had been born seven years previously. Between then and Patricia's and Martin's birth, two more sets (and a daughter) were born.

∽

THE *World of Wonders* (London, 1891) mentions a curious will from an undated copy of the *Dublin University Magazine*, which was set aside on the ground that the testator was *non compos mentis*. It ran as follows: 'Convinced that my dog has been the most faithful of my friends, I declare him the sole executor of this my last will and testament, and to him I trust the disposal of my fortune. I have great cause of complaint against the men: they are of no value, either physical or moral; my so-called friends false and perfidious. Of all the creatures that surround me I have found none to possess good qualities but Fidele. I dispose all of my property in his favour; and direct legacies may be given to all those on whom he voluntarily bestows his caresses, or distinguishes by wagging his tail.'

～

IN the 1860s the publisher Samuel Palmer toured southern Ireland and recorded this strange epitaph. Unfortunately, he did not note its location. Perhaps it still exists?

Bene	VI
AT. HT: HIS S. T.	Seab ATE yo
Oneli ESKA	VRG
THARI Neg Rayc	RIE Fan
Hang'd	DD
F.R.	Ryy O! V…Rey
O! mab V. Syli Fetol	Esf. OR. WH.
If. Ele	ATA
SS. CL.	wAi…Tsaflo
Ayb. Ye AR	O! Doft Ears W.
Th aN	Ho kNo wS.
Dcl –Ays	b uT
Hego	ina RVNO
Therp. Elfa	Fy Ears
ND	In.So…Metall-
NO WS. HE'stur	Pit…C
N'D Toe ART	Hero…R…broa
HH. Ersel Fy	D.P.
EWEE…Pin	ans.He…I
Gfr…I…En	N.H.
D.S.L.	Ers Hopma
Et mea D	Y.B.
	E.AG…AIN

For a long time, Palmer and his companions were puzzled by the enigmatic inscription. Was it some kind of archaic Latin code? After re-examining the epitaph, they noticed patterns emerging out of the cryptic text, and then the mystery was easily solved. This is what the inscription read:

Beneath this stone lies Katharine Gray,
Chang'd from a busy life to lifeless clay.
By earth and clay she got her pelf.
And now she's turn'd to earth herself.

Ye weeping friends – let me advise –
Abate your grief, and dry your eyes.
For what awaits a flood of tears?
Who knows, but, in a run of years,
In some small pitcher or broad pan
She in her shop may be again.

⤚

IN March 1927, Asagiro Sugetsugu, aged 22, became the first Japanese subject to be buried in Ireland. The sailor had died in an accident on board the steamship *Kinkasau Maru* and was buried in Cork.

⤚

THE following Lazarus-like resurrection of a sailor was reported in the *Dublin News-Letter* newspaper: 'On Sunday, 8 May [1743], a sailor was brought up from Rings End to Irish Town Churchyard to be buried; but when they laid him on the ground, the coffin was observed to stir, on which he was taken up; and by giving him some nourishment, he came to himself, and is likely to do well.'

⤚

ON 3 March 1780, news from County Tipperary set all of Ireland in wonder. The good people of Poinstown had seen strange apparitions in the sky. The sun sank bigger than it usually did and out of the west 'there stretched across the sky an arm of blue colour merging into black, and from its scarlet hand depended the shank of an anchor. Then sailing stern foremost there hove in sight moving northwards upon a dark smooth sea a frigate, her masts, sails and tackling and her crew clear to the naked eye.

'In another moment, amid scenes of confusion on deck, the sea swallowed her up. Next became visible a fort manned with a cannon. When the gun had spoken the fort changed into two vessels, which began to fight. The watchers could see the splash of bullets on the water until both ships foundered, and the last scene was of a sailor running desperately to the end of the bowsprit of the vessel, but unable to escape his death.

'After a little space came a small black chariot drawn by two horses. The chariot was pursued by a serpent to attack it, and, as it drew near to strike, a bull and a dog leaped from the chariot and, after a bloody tussle, worsted it.'

Was this a mirage or a mass hallucination? The event was never satisfactorily explained. Witnesses to this occurrence were very respectable people: a Mr Allye, a minister; a Lieutenant Dunsterville (his Christian name was Omen); Mr Bates, a schoolmaster; and a Mr Larkin. Yet the events seem too sensational to be true. Perhaps a more reasonable explanation is that the mirage may have had some basis in fact, but the observers gave free rein to their imagination in embellishing it.

⤜

32

TRISTRAM Shandy's famous author, Clonmel-born Laurence Sterne (1713–68), nearly lost his life in the waters of the Annamoe River in the Wicklow Mountains as a child. In 1720 Sterne was living in the barracks at Wicklow, where his father was stationed as a lieutenant in the army. The family received an invitation to stay at Annamoe Glebe with the rector, Rev. Fetherstone, who was a relative of his mother's. Laurence was only seven years old at the time. One day, while playing in the village, he fell into the millrace while the mill was working. By some stroke of luck, Sterne escaped without a scratch. The story of the child's adventure and miraculous survival spread through the district, and Sterne later related, with great gusto, how hundreds of the 'common people' had flocked to see him.

∽

THE origin of the phrase 'the Tenth don't dance' cannot be determined with certainty, but there is a consensus of opinion that it was uttered in a Dublin ballroom in the 19th century. As the story goes, it was when the 10th Hussars were stationed in Dublin in 1823/24 that the officers were invited to a ball given, some say, by the Lord Mayor. When the hostess offered to introduce the officers to ladies for dancing, they replied, 'The Tenth don't dance,' and she retorted, 'Then the Tenth can walk.' Another version has it that she made no reply, but later in the night said to a group of officers, 'Perhaps the Tenth don't sup?'

∽

JOHN O'Brien, a cadet of the Inchiquin family, had many hair's-breadth escapes during his career in the British Navy. He joined it in his early teens and was commissioned as a lieutenant in November 1747. The amazing adventure that earned him the nickname 'Sky Rocket Jack' shows how charmed a life he had. In 1747, he was fighting on board *HMS Dartmouth* against the Spanish man-of-war, the *Glorioso*, when, during the battle, a gunner ran up to him crying, 'Oh, sir, the powder room.' Then the ship blew up. O'Brien survived and was picked up, unconscious. The explosion, dreadful as it was, did not leave him with any lasting injuries and he remained in high spirits when he realised how lucky he had been. Introduced to the captain of the ship that had saved him, he addressed his rescuer with great gravity: 'Sir, you will excuse my appearing before you in these tattered and burned clothes; for I left my ship with such precipitation that I had not time to put on better ones.'

※

DR James Wolveridge of Cork is the author of what is said to be the oldest original work on midwifery by an English-speaking author. Published in London in 1671, *Speculum Matricis*, or the *Expert Midwives' Handmaid*, unusually takes the form of a dialogue between a doctor and a midwife.

※

IN Roderic O'Flaherty's account of west Connaught (*A Chorographical Description of West or H-Iar Connaught*), he mentions the spectacle of some fantastic ships in Galway Bay which appeared to be sailing against the wind in the sky. Mr Hardiman, who edited the manuscript in 1846 and was historian of Galway, was a little sceptical of this vision, which was believed to have occurred in 1161, until he watched a similar event with several other witnesses in

1798. He was on a hill near Croagh Patrick when the mirage of a fleet in full sail was seen in the sky. The aerial squadron was identified as that of Admiral Warren, who happened to have been pursuing some French vessels off the west coast at the same time.

∽

ON 2 February 1874, George Dawson saw a reflected rainbow at Balbriggan, County Dublin. The two legs of the aerial bow seemed only a few hundred yards away from the observer, and a reflection of the bow was seen in the water. The latter was evidently not an image of the bow in the air, because the two bows were not feet to feet. The reflected bow appeared to be lying inside the other, the red of the one commencing where the violet rays of the other disappeared.

∽

A 12-year-old boy who caught a baby that fell from the window ledge of a fourth-storey Dublin city centre flat was hailed as a hero for saving the infant's life. The incident occurred on the night of 31 August 1960 when 18-month-old Elizabeth McDermott crawled out on the window ledge of a flat in Phil Shanahan House, Sheriff Street. Liam Burke, who also lived in the flats and who was passing by, saw her topple. He dashed forward, thrust out his arms, and she fell into them. The baby was taken to Temple Street Children's Hospital, where she was detained for observation, suffering from shock. Elizabeth's grateful parents and neighbours presented Liam Burke with an inscribed watch as a token of their gratitude.

∽

THE Dublin Corporation band was first specifically mentioned in June 1561. At the conclusion of the mayoral banquet given by Thomas Fitzsimons, at which Lord Deputy Sussex was present, it was recorded: '…the Mayor and his brethren, with the city music, attended the Lord Deputy and Council to Thomas's Court by torchlight.' A rule was made by the Corporation in 1569/70 that the musicians 'shall serve in and throughout the city several days and nights every week, as time of year shall require.' Towards the end of Queen Elizabeth's reign, every householder in the city had to pay fourpence a year for the upkeep of the band. Each musician was granted 12 yards of blue cloth to make a livery. As the years rolled on, their privileges and their duties increased. In King Charles I's time, they were supposed to play through the city every night from October to February, and were also empowered to arrest 'all strange musicians' found playing in public.

∾

THE longest continuous herbaceous border in Ireland or Britain is in Strokestown Park Gardens, County Roscommon. It is 152.4 metres (500 feet) long.

∾

PUNISHMENT for criminal offences was much more severe in centuries past than it is now. For example, at the Antrim Assizes held in Carrickfergus on 16 March 1615, Ever McBrehon was condemned to be executed for having stolen a bridle worth five shillings, and Richy Bell suffered the same penalty, although the owner of the black horse which he had stolen was unknown. At the same Assizes it was decreed that two yeomen who on the previous

Christmas Eve had entered the house of 'a true and faithful subject', but did not get beyond the intention of committing burglary, should suffer the same extreme penalty for their bungling.

Another miscreant, one Donal Magee, got off lightly for stealing a goose. He was condemned to be whipped round the marketplace of Massereene, County Antrim and its surroundings. It was only during the reign of George IV that 'Grand Larceny' – that is, larceny above a shilling – ceased to be punishable by hanging.

∽

IN 1958, John O'Byrne, an 80-year old farmer from Glencolumbkille, County Donegal, cut over eight tons of turf and five tons of hay, unaided.

∽

FROM Kohat, on the borders of Afghanistan, comes an interesting tombstone epitaph of an Irish surgeon: 'Here rest the remains of Michael Healy, Apothecary in the Hon'ble Company's service, destroyed by the afreedees, 22nd March, 1850. Michael Healy was an Irishman, highly gifted with talents, energy and ambition. Foiled in his aim and weary of struggle with the world, he ardently sought that repose which he has here found.' The Afreedees were an Afghan tribe and the 'Hon'ble Company' mentioned was the Honourable East India Company.

∽

AN ill-starred attempt to establish a gunpowder factory at Clondalkin, County Dublin was made in the 18th century. A large factory built in 1783 by William Caldbeck was well on its way to becoming a prosperous concern when the mills were accidentally blown up in 1787. The shock of the explosion was felt in the city of Dublin and throughout a large part of the surrounding countryside. In Clondalkin, the effects were terrible. The entire building was destroyed and scattered over an area covering a quarter of a mile. Fish in the adjacent ponds were found dead, floating on the surface of the water. It is a testament to the builders of Clondalkin's 10th or 11th-century round tower that not a stone was dislodged by this explosion.

❧

THE largest ever teddy bears' picnic was attended by 33,573 bears and their owners at Dublin Zoo on 24 June 1995.

❧

IN an issue of the *Dublin Weekly Journal* for 1729, the following curious advertisement was displayed. It runs as follows: 'There is arrived in this City a High German, with a Flandrekin Hare, last from London, who has given unusual satisfaction to the Nobility and Gentry there. This Hare plays five Marches upon the Drum, 25 Exercises, and fights with a Dog to the Admiration of all Spectators. The said German will bring his Hare to any Gentlemen or Ladies who desire him to their Houses, giving him timely notice. His place of residence is at the Spread Eagle in Strand Street, near Capel Street.'

❧

PRESENT-day public functions compare poorly with what was considered normal in times past. An account survives of a breakfast given at the Rotunda in Dublin to the friends of the Marquis of Kildare towards the end of 1767. The record of the proceedings and the high-society notables present pales before the detailed statement of the delicacies provided for Kildare's guests. According to one source, these consisted of 100 rounds of beef, 100 neat [pickled ox] tongues, 100 sheep tongues, 100 baked pies, 100 sirloins of beef, 100 geese roasted, 100 turkeys roasted, 100 wild fowl, 100 ducks roasted, 100 pullets roasted, 1,000 French loaves, 2,000 large prints of butter, 100 weight of Gloucester cheese, tea, coffee, chocolate, 2,000 saffron cakes, 4,000 plain cakes, 50 hams, 2,500 bottles of wine, and a most splendid pyramid of sweetmeats in the middle of the dessert; likewise, a great number of stands of jelly and a curious fountain playing.

❧

A COPY of the *London Daily Post* dated 15 May 1731 contains an interesting article by its Dublin correspondent: 'A great difference happened this week between the students and fellows of our college, occasioned by the fixing of double penalties on those gentlemen who should stay out at night, which the scholars, imagining an unprecedented innovation, represented with such violence that two of them who were principally concerned were removed publickly: upon which were apprehended such dangerous consequences that it was thought necessary to compose matters in the easiest manner, and accordingly the two gentlemen were restored, and by the vigilance and industry of the Provost and Fellows everything is settled in the best way. The penalties were inflicted on account of the unhappy accident in which two watchmen were killed, the

Provost and Fellows thinking it advisable to take such measures to prevent future irregularities.'

᷒

AFTER floating about in the sea for 19 years, a scarred and discoloured lifebelt, marked *SS Titanic*, washed ashore at Gravesend Bay, New York on 29 May 1931. The Belfast-built White Star liner sank on 15 April 1912 after a collision with an iceberg off Newfoundland. Over 1,500 lives were lost.

᷒

AFTER World War I, Irishman James Kelly emigrated to New York. By the time of his retirement in 1959, 'Smelly' Kelly, as he was known, was a famous figure in his adopted city. It was Kelly's nose that made him famous. He had a peculiar talent for finding obscure gas and water leaks and acquired a well-earned reputation for being an expert in his field. For 34 years it was his job to patrol the tracks on the IND (Independent) Division of the New York subway system, searching out leaks. It was a vital job. Water leaks could cause cave-ins and seeping fumes could be ignited by a single spark, causing explosion, fire, destruction and death. Kelly hiked all 723 miles of track, averaging about 10 miles a day for a total of nearly 90,000 miles, sniffing every step of the way. Usually he found eight leaks a day.

᷒

IN a letter to a correspondent, the famous Irish beauty Mrs Delany wrote in January 1758: 'Does Mary cough in the night? Two or three snails boiled in her barley water, or tea water or whatever she drinks, might be of some service to her. Taken in time they have done wonderful cures; she must know something of it. They give no manner of taste. It would be best nobody should know of it but yourself. I should imagine six or eight boiled in a quart of water, and skimmed off and put in a bottle would be a good way, adding a spoonful or two of that to every liquid she takes. They must be fresh done every two or three days; otherwise they grow thick.'

∽

A WEALTHY French nobleman was captivated by the spectacular Marino Casino during a trip to Dublin in September 1964 and announced his intention to build an exact replica at his estate near Paris. The Marquis de Beostegul marvelled at the 18th-century building's splendid architectural design, falling in love with it at first sight. *The Irish Times* estimated that it would cost as much as £300,000 to build an exact copy.

∽

DURING the Dark Ages, it was dangerous to express the opinion that the earth might be spherical, not flat. In the early 8th century, a geographer named Feargil left Ireland and joined the court of King Pepin in France. Feargil, Latinised into Virgilus, became a favourite of the king, who recommended him to Otho, Duke of Bavaria, for the Bishopric of Salzburg. After two years' probation in that province, Virgilus was consecrated as bishop in the year 767. Some time afterwards, he published a treatise on the antipodes, in which he described the earth as a sphere, contrary to the Ptolemaic doctrine, which held that it was a flat disc of land surrounded by a great river known as Oceanus. The authorities denounced this unorthodox view and acted quickly. The unfortunate Hibernian philosopher was summoned before a tribunal, found guilty of heresy and was burned at the stake.

≈

WHILE fishing off the coast of north Mayo in October 1927, fishermen from Inniskea caught more than they had bargained for when a large whale became entangled in their nets. While trying to save their property, several fishermen narrowly escaped drowning. As the whale thrashed about, trying to free itself, it became more entangled. Fearing for their lives, the fishermen fled the scene, but cautiously returned to find that the whale had died and its very valuable carcass was floating on the surface.

≈

GEORGE Bernard Shaw was a brilliant writer and wit. He was master of the put-down and usually had the last word. But there were a few occasions when he was bested. He certainly met his match in young New York reporter Marjorie Harrison, who was sent to interview the great man in 1931, because he was well known for providing good 'copy'. She tracked him down to a circus in New York and tried to interview him. Shaw was less than co-operative.

When she tried to engage him, asking about how he liked the lions, he briskly dismissed her, saying, 'My dear girl, I see no good reason why I should give you material for an article for which you will receive 15 shillings, when I may write it and get five hundred pounds.'

Marjorie Harrison evidently was made of stern stuff, and got her article and revenge on the reluctant interviewee. She merely wrote an account of her failed interview and concluded it as follows: 'Mr. Shaw wants five hundred pounds sterling for his opinion of the lions. The lions, however, gave their opinion of Mr. Shaw for nothing. They sat back and yawned.'

∽

ACCORDING to the *Hibernian Magazine* of 1864, the dangerous sport of 'shooting' the falls on the River Shannon was once a favourite pastime of the local fishermen. The Falls of Doonass, one of the beauty-spots of the river, were the scene of these exploits, and the craft chosen was a very light skiff. In the bows stood a man with a long pole to steer the boat, while at the same time, by careful balancing, he manipulated the boat. The fishermen became so skilful at this risky hobby that few accidents occurred. Sometimes, however, they carried passengers, and then a sudden nervous movement might upset the frail shell, in which case, as the author of the article remarked, 'swimming would be of no avail'.

∽

HIGHWAYMEN infested the Irish countryside for many centuries until the authorities all but wiped them out in the early 19th century. Usually they robbed the wealthy and lined their own pockets with the spoils. Some were violent and cruel, others were dashing and stylish – gentlemen highwaymen – and seem closer to the romantic rogues of fiction than a grasping thief.

The politest robbery on record in Ireland was made by an unknown highwayman in the Phoenix Park, Dublin in August 1776. A lady and her servant were enjoying a ride through the park when they were stopped by a man on foot. The man was startlingly well dressed, in a white suit and a gold-laced hat. He demanded the lady's money. She had 26 guineas and gave it to him without hesitation. After pocketing the cash, he took a small diamond hoop ring from another pocket and presented it to the pretty woman. He told her to wear it for his sake, because the highwayman made it a point of honour to take no more from a beautiful lady than he could make a return for in value. He then politely bowed and, vaulting over a wall, disappeared.

~

THE 1832 volume of the *Dublin Penny Magazine* describes a murder solved by a dream. Ulick Maguire, a farmer, had given shelter and food for some time to a poor idiotic cousin. One night, Ulick's wife dreamed that her husband was murdered, and the dream was associated with the house of a rejected lover of hers, named O'Flanagan. She told this to a neighbour's wife. Soon after, the cousin, to whom it had not been told, began chanting the strange incidents of that dream in a doggerel rhyme.

On the following night, the husband actually was murdered, and when the idiot awoke in the morning, he cried out in terror, 'Shamus dhub More [Big Black James] O'Flanagan has kilt Ulick, and buried him under the new ditch at the back of the garden. I dhramed it last night, ivry wurd of it.' A search was made at the spot indicated, and the body of poor Ulick was found, with the skull cleft in two. It was soon found that O'Flanagan had absconded.

He enlisted, but being traced and arrested, he confessed to the crime and was executed.

∽

SIX members of the Doyle family of Gortboy, near the Gap of Dunloe in County Kerry, were put in Killarney lunatic asylum in January 1888 after the savage murder of a 13-year-old imbecile family member. When police arrived on the scene, the family – Michael Doyle (a well-to-do farmer), his wife, four sons and three daughters – were in a frenzied state and acting like violent lunatics. Some of them were naked and carrying pitchforks, while the boy's corpse lay on a dung pit, along with bedclothes and other items from the house. After much resistance, the police managed to capture the family and gain control of the macabre situation.

∽

IN September 1964, newspapers reported that the only lovers' lane left in Cookstown, County Tyrone was to remain unlighted. When the local urban council was considering an application for street lights on the roadway, an official stated that it was the only roadway in the district along which young people could court. A member, Mr Robert Vaughn, remarked, 'Don't let us spoil it.' The other councillors agreed and Tullagh Lane was to remain in darkness. 'Lights out in Lovers' Lane' was the predictable newspaper headline.

∽

IN times past it was customary for prisoners to pay rent for their lodging and upkeep in some Irish jails. This was certainly the case in the 'Black Dog', adjacent to the New-gate Prison in Dublin, which was used to detain debtors and those awaiting trial. It comprised 12 rooms containing beds. Each prisoner had to pay the keeper one shilling a night, even though there were four or five sharing the same bed! Those who were unable to pay this fee were thrown into a dungeon, known ironically as the 'Nunnery', because prostitutes arrested by the watch were confined there. Its only window opened into the side of a common sewer, which frequently flooded the floor of the cell. It is recorded that when Edmond Donnelly, a city merchant, was committed there for debt, the water often rose to the level of his bed, which rotted under him.

The most notorious of the keepers of the 'Black Dog' was John Hawkins, who had paid his predecessor £245 for his goodwill of the office, as well as a gratuity of £100 to the mayor and sheriffs for the privilege. Rents, fees and sale of liquor to the prisoners brought him and his wife an income of £1,163 a year until he was eventually appre-hended by the Sergeant-at-Arms for 'extortion, great cor-ruption, and treating the prisoners with the utmost cruelty and barbarity'. It was alleged that he had even kept in prison many citizens who had not been lawfully commit-ted by a magistrate.

❧

QUEEN Elizabeth I unwittingly made a Mayo widow a 'captain' with the right to retain 20 armed men, paid for by the royal treasury. Castlekirke, or the 'Hen's Castle', is an ivied ruin situated on a narrow spit of land that juts out into the Corrib near Maam Bridge. During Queen Eliza-beth's reign, an heiress of the O'Flahertys, who was a widow with an only daughter, shut herself up in the castle with 20 loyal followers to protect her property from the greed of her own family and that of the neighbouring Burke clan. In order to regularise her position and render it even more secure from aggression, she wrote to the Queen asking permission to arm her followers on account of the disturbed condition of the country.

The letter, according to the fashion of the time, was signed with her maiden name, Bevinda O'Flaherty. The Queen, not being familiar with Irish Christian names, seems to have thought her petitioner was a man because in her reply she authorises 'her good friend, Captain Bevinda O'Flaherty' to maintain 20 armed men, at her Majesty's expense, for the peace of the country. The story of Captain Bevinda and her beautiful daughter is the subject matter of Maurice Walsh's stirring novel *Blackcock's Feather*.

જી

THERE was a penny post service in Dublin many years before it was introduced across Britain and Ireland in 1840. The 'General Penny Post Office' had 90 'receiving offices' within the city and suburbs. By all accounts, it was an excellent service that has never been bettered. It is best described in the 1824 edition of *Wilson's Dublin Directory*: 'So secure and expeditious is the dispatch and delivery of letters by this Office, that two persons residing in the most distant parts of the City, may, between seven o'clock in the morning and eight o'clock in the evening, write four letters and receive three answers in the Day, and the answer to the fourth by nine next morning, for the trifling expense of one Penny on each.'

જી

THE first memorial to be erected in Britain or Ireland celebrating Nelson's victory at the Battle of Trafalgar was erected in Castletownshend, County Cork. When the news of the great victory of Trafalgar reached Cork, Captain Watson, then commander of the Sea Fencibles, proceeded at once to build a suitable memorial arch with the assistance of his men and a few masons. This memorial to the great admiral was built upon the summit of a high hill in Castletownshend demesne over a remarkably short period. The marble tablet embedded in it bore the following inscription: 'This arch, the first monument erected to the memory of Nelson after the Battle of Trafalgar, was sketched and planned by Captain Joshua Watson, R.N., and built by him and 1,200 of the Sea Fencibles, then under his command. It was erected in five hours on the 10th November, 1805.'

❧

IN the summer of 1954, Youghal, County Cork was transformed into the whaling port of New Bedford, Massachusetts of a century before when the ancient town was used to film scenes for the film *Moby Dick*, starring Gregory Peck. The old quay front was altered to look like something out of a history book. Tall-masted schooners, timbered buildings, outsize barrels and fierce-looking characters all added reality to the created illusion of the filmmakers. One man who long remembered Youghal for its wonderful co-operation was Charles Parker, the film's make-up expert.

When he arrived in Youghal, he was faced with a very serious problem that threatened to hold up the production.

The make-up of the amazingly tattooed face of the character Queequeg – the royal-blooded savage of the South Seas (actually played by an Austrian actor, Friedrich Ledebur) – consisted of a special skin-tight mask. Parker and his staff spent three months researching and developing these special masks. They finally succeeded in making a mould of the required tattoo, but before sufficient masks could be moulded, the unit had to leave England for Youghal, but Parker had only a few of the masks available. Just when he thought he would have to return to England to make more, which would mean holding up the production, a local company came to the rescue.

When he heard of the film's problem, Michael Swarbrick, who managed Seafield Fabrics (a nylon manufacturer in Youghal), immediately put his firm's laboratories at Parker's disposal. Through the engineering skill of the factory electrician, Mike Culhane, a special oven was rewired to achieve and maintain the required temperature, and it proved a success in moulding the masks.

A local boy, Oliver Russell, was trained to make the masks, and as many as five of them were turned out daily, with the result that Queequeg's tattoos for the remainder of the film were Irish-made. The trio's efforts were a major contribution to *Moby Dick*. The director, John Huston, summed it up best: 'Our needs were many, our demands were unexpected, and our time strictly limited, but the people of Youghal stayed with us all the way through. My finest tribute to them is simply: Nobody could have done better, and their great spirit of co-operation and hospitality will be clearly reflected in Youghal's part in the production of *Moby Dick*.'

శ్రీ

JOHN Barrow's *A Tour Round Ireland* (1835) contains a passage in which he relates that while travelling in the west of Ireland, he found a noticeboard in an orchard which said 'Bewar of Sneks'. This, he explains, meant 'beware of snakes'; however, these snakes were not the species driven out by St Patrick, but a kind of man-trap. A long iron spike, well barbed, was fitted into a block of wood which was then buried in an orchard. What happened when a thief trod on the barbed spike can be left to the imagination. Barrow comforted his readers by saying that in this case the bark was worse than the bite, and that as far as he could make out, the warning was generally fictitious, the owner trusting that it would be sufficient to frighten off any potential thieves.

≈

THE following ingenious letter was published in *The Dublin Penny Journal* of 7 June 1834, presumably a long time after it had been written. A newlywed young lady, who had to show her husband all the letters she wrote, composed it. She outwitted her husband and sent this letter to a close friend:

> I cannot be satisfied, my Dearest friend:
> blest as I am in the matrimonial state,
> unless I pour into your friendly bosom
> which has ever beat in unison with mine,
> the various sentiments which swell
> with the liveliest emotions of pleasure,
> my almost bursting heart. I tell you my dear
> husband is the most amiable of men.
> I have now been married seven weeks, and

have never found the least reason to
repent the day that joined us. My husband is
both in person and manners far from resembling
ugly, cross, old, disagreeable, and jealous
monsters, who think by confining to secure;
a wife it is his maxim to treat as a
bosom friend, ------------------ and not as a
play-thing, or menial slave, the woman
of his choice ------------------ neither party,
he says, should always obey implicitly,
but each yield to the other by turns.
An ancient maiden aunt, near seventy,
a cheerful, venerable, and pleasant old lady
lives in the house with us – she is the de-
light of both young and old; she is civil to all the neighbourhood round,
generous and charitable to the poor.
I am convinced my husband likes nothing more
than he does me; he flatters me more
than the glass, and his intoxication,
(for so I must call the excess of his love),
often makes me blush for the unworthiness
of its object, and wish I could be more deserving
of the man whose name I bear. To
say all in one word ---------- and to
crown the whole, ---------- my former lover
is now my indulgent husband, my fondness
is returned, and I might have had
a Prince without the felicity I find in
him. Adieu! May you be as blest as I am unable to wish that I could be more
happy!

N.B. – The key to the above letter (in cipher) is to read the first, and then every alternate line only.

❧

THE following letter was published in *The Irish Times* of 13 October 1931. The editor refrained from making any comment except to say that the writer had assured him of the veracity of what he had described: 'At the hotel in which I was staying in Nenagh last week a party of men arrived by car bearing with them a cage which housed an animal phenomenon in the form of a cross between a rat and a rabbit. The beast was little larger than a rat, had a rat's tail, ears and claws. Its skin and head were those of a rabbit. The eyes are too timid to be those of a rat, but they are too small for a rabbit's.

'The animal walks like a rat, and holds food between its claws as a rat, but nibbles like a rabbit. Food is a problem; for, while the rat-rabbit will eat meat in plenty, it cannot get along without green vegetables. The birthplace, or at least the home, of this extraordinary animal was in a field near Clonmel, where it was discovered by some children, who raised the "alarm". It took a dozen men some time to effect its capture, although it is now quite timid both in and out of its cage. I commend to the ingenious the task of finding a suitable name for this curious specimen.'

❧

ERECTED in 1863 after the death of Colonel Maurice Dennis of Bermingham House, the nearby Dennis Mausoleum of Clonbern, County Galway is probably unique in Ireland because it is made entirely of cast iron. This splendid example of the Victorian celebration of death can best be described as biscuit-barrel shaped. It is ornamented with wonderfully elaborate classical features.

᥊

IN late 1735, *The Gentleman's Magazine* included the following bizarre report: 'Nov. 28. From Ireland. A man about 18 inches high, cover'd with strong hair, was lately taken in a field near Longford by a farmer, of whom the little gentleman demanded why he be stopped, for he was travelling for the north in order to pass over for Scotland, but all his entreaties could not produce him liberty, the farmer having been at the expense of a box to carry him about, and to make a show of him. He speaks Irish and mimics English.'

᥊

MAURICE Burton's Animal Legends (1955) includes a cutting from *The Irish Times* about that legendary sight, a stoat's funeral. It was seen by a professional man in County Mayo, who 'was driving from Balla to Claremorris when he noticed what he thought was a monster snake crossing the road. He slowed speed, and, on approaching the "object", found that it was a procession of stoats. In front were four carrying the body, and behind them came nearly a hundred other stoats, two by two. When the "mourners" had crossed the road, climbed a fence and entered the field, the car-driver followed them, but left them when some of them…began to spit at him.'

᥊

IN an unnamed country parish magazine from the 1930s, the following gem of unintentional humour appeared:

'A jumble sale will be held in the Parochial Hall on the second Saturday of the month. This is a chance for the ladies of the parish to get rid of anything that is not worth keeping, but is too good to be thrown away. Don't forget to bring your husbands.'

∽

A WOLF was said to have terrorised sheep in Counties Cavan, Limerick and Clare in 1874. According to a correspondent of *Land and Water* (7 March 1874), the depredations had caused 'terrible losses for poor people'. Another correspondent wrote to say that in 42 incidents known to him, the sheep were killed in a vampire-ish manner, throats torn and blood sucked or lapped. Large, dog-like footprints, similar to those of a dog but more elongated, gave rise to the belief in a ravaging wolf, although no one had seen the creature.

In April, Archdeacon Magenniss shot a large dog and claimed he had rid the land of its evildoer. It did not work. According to the *Clare Journal* for late April, the killings continued. A second dog was shot to no effect, but eventually the number of deaths declined until they stopped altogether. Nevertheless, around the same time, a second series of sheep killings was in progress over a hundred miles away, in County Limerick, carried out by 'a wolf or something like it'. It was said that several people bitten by the animal had been taken to Ennis asylum, 'labouring under strange symptoms of insanity'. Although this does sound like the work of a rabid dog, the killings in Cavan were never explained nor the killer identified.

∽

PIRATES were one of the greatest dangers to shipping crossing the Irish Sea in the 17th century. A Dutch captain named De Ruyter, sailing from Dublin to Holland with a cargo of butter, found himself pursued by a pirate vessel. The Dutch ship was unarmed, but the captain decided to attempt to outwit his enemies. He ordered his men to take off their boots and stockings, break open several butter casks and spread the contents over the deck of the ship. The pirates came alongside, and De Ruyter, assuming an air of feigned submission, allowed them to come aboard the merchantman.

But when the pirates jumped over, fully armed with cutlasses and pistols, they slipped about and tumbled over one another on the buttery deck. One fellow slid into a cabin, where he was immediately sat on by the ship's boy. Another shot across the deck and out into the sea via an opposite porthole. Not one of them could stand, and being, like all pirates, intensely superstitious, they cried out that the ship was possessed by the devil. In a hurried retreat, the pirates cast loose and De Ruyter got safely into port, thanks to a few barrels of butter.

❧

THE poem 'On the Burial of Sir John Moore' was an instant classic elegy on the death of the Commander of the British forces in the Peninsular War when it was first published in the *Newry Telegraph* on 19 April 1817. Yet its author, the Rev. Charles Wolfe, curate of Donaghmore, County Tyrone, never claimed its authorship. During his life, it was ascribed to many authors (Byron among them), but it was only the discovery of a letter after his death which proved that Wolfe had written it.

This strange man lived in a state of absolute poverty. A few rickety chairs and a small table, all heaped with books and papers, were his only furniture. Two trunks served as cupboards and also to cover the holes in the floor. The wallpaper hung in long, mouldering strips. He rarely bothered to eat anything more than a crust. This way of life rapidly undermined his health and he died from tuberculosis in Cork, aged only thirty-one. Wolfe, who was born in Blackhall, County Kildare, is remembered for this one poem.

∽

PIRACY, smuggling and wrecking were once the main occupations along the rugged, rocky south coast of Ireland. In the 1920s, an 'eminently respectable' friend of *The Irish Times* editor Robert Smyllie, who lived on the coast near Courtmacsherry, County Cork, surprised Smyllie by recounting how his ancestors used to make a great deal of money 'wrecking'. A simple but ingenious method was used to lure unsuspecting ships to their doom on the rugged coastline. At night, lanterns were attached to the horns of cattle grazing on top of the cliffs. Approaching vessels, mistaking the moving lights for Kinsale or Cork Harbour, would turn in towards land and immediately be wrecked on the reefs. Casks of liquor and miscellaneous goods would float ashore, though occasionally the unlucky ship remained sufficiently intact to be boarded and plundered by the local opportunists. All the local villagers were involved in the despicable enterprise. The wildness of the countryside paralysed the law, and for a long period this lucrative business thrived.

∽

CRUMLIN was one of the four ancient manors in the County Dublin which were the property of the Crown, and in the Holinshed Chronicles (1577), we read the following quaint notice of it as such:

'The Manor of Crumlin payeth a greater chief rent to the prince than any of the other three, which proceedeth of this: the Seneschal [Administrator], being offended with the tenants for their misdemeanour, took them up very sharply in the court, and with rough and minatory speeches, began to menace them. The lobbish and desperate clobberiousness, taking the matter in dudgeon, made no more words, but knocked their Seneschal on the costard, and left him there, sprawling on the ground for dead. For which detestable murder their rent was enhanced, and they pay at this day ninepence per acre, which is double to any of the other three Manors.'

⊰

COUNTY Carlow can boast that it has Ireland's, and indeed Europe's, largest megalithic cromlech. This huge boulder is to be found at Kernanstown, or Brown's Hill, in the north of the county. It is 23 feet long, 22 feet wide, about 65 feet in girth, and is estimated to weigh 100 tons. How such an enormous mass of stone was raised remains a mystery.

⊰

ON 7 June 1978, the then President of Ireland, Patrick Hillery, received a surprise present on behalf of the people of Ireland when the producer of the film *The Great Train Robbery* unexpectedly made a gift of the 15-carriage

Victorian train used in the film. The period train – worth £82,000 at the time – was built over three months at the National Film Studios in Bray, County Wicklow. The restored steam engine and specially built carriages were central to the film's plot, which was based on the first train robbery in history, where daring thieves snatched £25,000 in gold from an English train in 1855.

The film's producer, John Foreman, presented the train to President Hillery at an exclusive lunch attended by Princess Grace and Prince Rainier of Monaco. President Hillery could only express his thanks and exclaim, 'What does one say when one is given a gift of a train?'

❧

WHEN the Hon. Desmond Guinness and Princess Marie-Gabrielle von Urach Württemberg got married at Christ Church Cathedral, Oxford on 3 July 1954, they had one unexpected guest. Sixty-year-old Patrick O'Reilly, a dustman from Dublin, was invited to the wedding by mistake when he had sent a letter of congratulation after hearing of the forthcoming marriage. He hired a morning suit and top hat for the occasion and even sent the bride a shamrock for good luck. With a white carnation in his buttonhole, the Dubliner attended the ceremony and was made very welcome by the Guinnesses once they realised what had happened. When O'Reilly arrived at the ceremony, he told reporters, 'I am very glad to be here, though it all seems very strange for a working man.'

❧

IRISHMEN were the first soldiers to win Victoria Crosses in both World Wars. Lieutenant Maurice James

Dease of Turbotstown House, Coole, County Westmeath was posthumously awarded the VC as a result of his heroic actions on 23 August 1914 when four German battalions launched themselves against Nimy Bridge in Belgium, which was being defended by a single company and only one machine gun, manned by Lieutenant Dease. Despite being shot five times, the brave Irish soldier stuck to his guns, raining down deadly fire on the enemy. Dease was later rescued, but died of his wounds.

Captain Harold Marcus Ervine-Andrews from Keadue, County Cavan was awarded the first VC of World War II. During the night of 31 May 1940 near Dunkirk, France, his company was attacked by an overwhelming German force. They managed to inflict heavy enemy casualties before he led his remaining unwounded men back to safety, wading for over a mile in water up to their chins. Captain Ervine-Andrews returned home after the war but was driven out by the IRA. He moved to England and pursued a successful military career, achieving the rank of Lieutenant Colonel. The last surviving Irish holder of the VC to die, he passed away in 1995, aged eighty-three.

෴

ATHLONE-born Thomas Flinn (1842–92) was one of the two youngest winners of the distinguished Victoria Cross medal (at 15 years and three months). The other winner was Andrew Fitzgibbon (1845–83), who was born in India of Irish parentage. It cannot be established which of them was the younger winner, because Flinn's birth date in August 1842 it not known. Flinn was a drummer in the 64th Regiment (later the North Staffordshire Regiment – the Prince of Wales's) during the Indian Mutiny of 1857, when he earned his award. On 28 November that year at Cawnpore, during a charge on the enemy's guns, Drummer Flinn (although wounded) fought hand-to-hand with two of the enemy artillerymen.

❧

LURGAN-born William Miller was a late 18th-century portrait and landscape painter (who sometimes painted on glass). He also invented what must have been an early speaking clock – 'a life size figure of a man who could articulate sounds and call out the hours of the clock'. It was modelled as the figure of an old man standing in a case. When he could not find a buyer, Miller dismantled it.

❧

THE Cork Medley newspaper contains a sea yarn that deserves to be rescued from obscurity. Their Kinsale correspondent reported on 4 June 1738: 'Some time ago Capt. John Madox, Commander of the *Charming Sally*, of Bristol, on his passage home from Guinea and Jamaica, about 300 leagues westward of Ireland, unfortunately struck against a grampus of prodigious size, which was, as supposed, sleeping. The ship gave a terrible bounce, surprised all hands, and overset chests, etc. in the cabin and between decks.

'As it was by day they plainly saw the fish, and believe the ship's keel when she ran over it cut it in a very terrible manner, the sea being all stained with its blood. The ship immediately complained, and on finding her to make water, to prevent her foundering, they stuffed in pieces of beef and pork between the planks, and so by continual pumping kept her above the water for five days, when they happily espied a sail. The captain had just time to bring off his gold and gold dust and some provisions till their arrival in Cork.'

ക

DUBLIN-born John Oldham (1779–1840) was a renowned miniature painter and the inventor of a machine that numbered bank notes individually. This invention was rejected by the Newry Bank but was adopted by the Bank of Ireland in 1812. Oldham also invented 'a set of paddles driven by steam for propelling ships at sea', and the first seagoing iron-clad steamship was fitted with these paddles.

ക

ON the edge of a river in County Cavan it is alleged that there was once a stone with the following inscription: 'N.B. When this stone is out of sight, it is not safe to ford the river.'

ക

DUBLIN doctor Jonathan Osborne (1794–1864) had himself buried in an upright coffin because 'at the resurrection he would not like anyone to have an advantage over him. He had arthritic hips.'

ക

'LEGLESS Man's Feat of Arms' was the tabloid-like headline in an old copy of *The Irish Times*. The accompanying article concerned a legless man who 'walked' through the streets of Dundalk on his hands on 12 March 1927. He was followed by a large crowd who could not quite believe their eyes. The man wore sandals on his hands and was accompanied by a goat, harnessed to a small cart, containing camping equipment and cooking utensils.

Civic Guards were on hand to regulate the traffic and crowds and so enable the athlete to proceed on his way. He was said to be an ex-officer of a Canadian regiment who had lost both his legs in World War I and had undertaken to walk from Dublin to Belfast for a bet.

∽

SOME TIME in 1729, according to an account in *Walsh's Impartial News-Letter*, Dublin was overrun by rats. The article says, 'This morning we have an account from Merian of these outlandish Marramounts that are called Mountain rats, who are grown so very common that they walk in droves and do a great deal of mischief; people have killed several which are as big as Kats and Rabbits. This part of the country is infested with them; the like Vermin destroyed a little child in the field. Likewise we hear from Rathfarnham that they are to be seen like rabbits, and are so impudent that they attempt strange things. Nay, abundance of them are to be seene in Fleet Street.'

∽

THE barrister and orator John Philpot Curran (1750–1817) invented a highly effective, but impractical, alarm clock when he was a student. Writing to a friend, he said, 'I have contrived a machine after the manner of an hourglass, which, perhaps, you may be curious to know, awakes me regularly at half-past four. Exactly over my head I have suspended two vessels of tin, one above the other. When I go to bed, which is always at ten, I pour a bottle of water into the upper vessel, in the bottom of which is a hole of such size as to let the water pass through so as to make the inferior reservoir overflow in six hours and a half. I have had no small trouble in proportioning these vessels; and I was still more puzzled, for a while, how to confine my head so as to receive the drop; but I have at length succeeded.'

∽

ON 2 April 1752, William and Thomas Fitzgerald were executed at Broadlane, Cork for robbing one William Keating of six shillings. While William was on trial at city-court, his brother Thomas (who was also accused of the robbery but not captured), being conscious of his own innocence, carried a quart of ale into the open court and gave it to his brother in the dock. He was immediately captured, tried by the same jury, found guilty and then executed along with his brother.

∽

A KILLER hanged in 1888 is still legally alive to this day. Dr William Cross from Cork was convicted of poisoning his first wife, sentenced to death and later hanged – but he is still legally alive. As the law then stood, a jury was sworn in to assist the prison governor in carrying out the death sentence by viewing the body of the executed man and certifying death. By custom, however, the jury had ceased to view the body. They took the word of the governor and prison doctor and certified accordingly. On this occasion, though, a strongly nationalist jury refused to take the governor's word and he in turn refused to show them the body, on the grounds that it had already been in quicklime for some hours. The jury therefore refused to certify death.

∽

THREE burglars who raided a home in Castleknock, County Dublin in early April 1978 did not expect the warm reception they received at the hands of Lawrence and Kathryn Power and their 17-year-old son Larry. Tipperary man Lawrence Power was awakened from his sleep when he heard the burglars discussing what they should steal.

He woke his wife, then raced downstairs to confront the thieves. Startled by the sudden appearance of the sturdy 44-year-old homeowner, the trio dropped the valuables they were collecting and bolted through French windows and down the back garden. One escaped and another was attacked by Mrs Power as he tried to scale a wall, but he too eventually fled. The unluckiest of the fleeing men fell into the swimming pool. Lawrence Power tackled the drenched intruder. There was a fierce struggle and it took a lot of effort to subdue the thief at the poolside. The couple's son, woken by the fracas, helped his father overpower the soaked, battered burglar with the liberal use of a hurley stick.

Neighbours, awakened by the noise, quickly arrived to help restrain the defeated burglar. A short while later the would-be thief was relieved to see the gardaí arriving to rescue him. In hospital, it emerged that he had a broken nose and a suspected fractured skull. Gardaí also arrested another badly cut and bruised man in a nearby laneway.

The third man escaped without a scratch, but was later discovered at home hiding under his bed.

๑

IN late September 1959, Matthew Morrissey of Newtown, Kilmuckridge, County Wexford landed a pike weigthing 15 ½ lb when fishing in the Ballinahoun River. When the fish was opened, it was found to contain a full-sized wild duck.

๑

JOHN Lewis, a Dublin artist, invented the first painted 'drop scene' in the 1770s. This appeared in Crow Street Theatre, Dublin, when Drury Lane and other London theatres were still using the time-honoured green curtains. They quickly adopted Lewis's idea and it is still a standard feature in many theatres.

๑

A FEW hours after flying into Ireland in May 1960 from his native Kenya, Rory Rudd was fighting for his life after being bitten by one of the deadliest of all African snakes. The 19-year-old had arrived in the country to study at Trinity College, Dublin. He brought a young burrowing viper with him in a cigarette tin. Rory had owned it for five months and had decided to present it to Dublin Zoo. When he opened the tin at the zoo, he caught the live end, instead of lifting it out by the tail, and the snake bit him.

Rory's thumb quickly turned black and his arm swelled. His uncle, Dr Harry Wright of Mount Merrion, immediately started a frantic search for viper serum. After several phone calls, it was discovered that London Zoo had recently taken possession of two precious ampoules from its counterpart in Johannesburg, South Africa. The serum was flown to Dublin in record time. Rory finally received the life-saving treatment 11 hours after he had been bitten.

He had to have part of his thumb removed because of gangrene, but was otherwise little the worse for wear when he spoke to reporters from his bed in Sir Patrick Dun's Hospital a few days later. His only concern was whether or not doctors would allow him out to sit the entrance examination for the Faculty of Engineering in Trinity College a few days later. In spite of his experience, Rory intended to have another and larger snake – a python – sent to Dublin to present it to Dublin Zoo. His pet burrowing viper was not so lucky – it had to be destroyed because Dublin Zoo did not then keep poisonous reptiles.

❧

THE bugle that sounded the famous Charge of the Light Brigade at Balaclava in 1854 during the Crimean War was made in McNeill's music shop at 140 Capel Street, Dublin. For many years the mould on which the bell of the bugle was made was on display in the shop.

❧

DURING the raging of the plague in Dublin in 1604/05, it was ordered that 'for better purging of the air every inhabitant should burn a faggot [a bundle of sticks] at his door on the nights of Mondays, Wednesdays, and Saturdays'.

❧

THE state of Pennsylvania in the United States is not named after its famous Quaker founder, William Penn. It is in fact named after his father, Cork-born Admiral William Penn. In Penn's own account of the naming of the colony (found in his letter to Robert Turner of 5 January 1681), he wrote, 'And they added Penn to it and though I much opposed it and went to the king to have it struck out and altered, he said it was past and he would take it upon him, for I feared lest it should be looked on as a vanity in me. But the king said, "We will keep it, but not on your account, my dear fellow, don't flatter yourself. We will keep the name to commemorate the Admiral, your noble father."'

Ironically, Admiral Penn was a bitter opponent of Quakerism, and on one occasion whipped, beat and turned his son out of doors for listening to the preachings of Thomas Loe, a Quaker.

༄

A FANG-tooth of a wolf was used in Ireland up to the early part of the 18th century to help children cut their teeth. They were usually set in silver or gold. A letter dated March 1713 from Lady Isabella Wentworth to her son, Lord Strafford, mentions this custom: 'I have made your daughter a present of a wolf's tooth. I sent to Ireland for it, and set it here in gold. They are very lucky things; for of my first two one did die, the other bred his very ill, and none of the rest did, for I had one for all the rest.'

༄

THERE was at one time a leper settlement in Galway. In the old church of St Nicholas in that city there is a lepers' gallery, high up, close to the vaulting of the roof. Here, by private access, the unfortunate victims of this dreadful scourge were allowed to join in public worship.

❧

SOME time in January 1722 an unnamed Dublin newspaper carried a description of an 'eruption which happened on the banks of the Liffey, on the back of Blessingtown'. The writer stated that 'about 100 yards of ground, containing a potato garden, and a boy sitting thereon, with a pitcher of buttermilk, observing rabbits playing on a neighbouring hill, at once was lifted up and thrown about 40 yards across the river, and there rested on the opposite bank, all the while the boy, holding fast by a bunch of rushes, was, with the pile of ground, left safe there.'

❧

A MODERN-day medical miracle occurred in November 2005 when 80-year-old Frank Tighe from Streete, County Westmeath saw his wife Bridget for the first time in 60 years after an operation allowed him to see again. He owed his good fortune to the brilliant medical staff at Dublin's Eye and Ear Hospital. They successfully restored vision to Frank's right eye with a cornea transplant. But why he suddenly had lost his sight 60 years before still remains a mystery. He went to bed one night as a healthy young man and woke up blind.

Frank and his family were delighted with his regained vision. Seeing his wife after 60 years and seeing his sons, grandchildren and great-grandchildren for the very first time was his greatest thrill. In an interview with *The Sun* on 1 December, Frank admitted, 'I'm a new man. It is a whole new world for me. Everything is so different. I just can't believe the lovely scenery and all the houses.'

∽

IN the 1760s, James McAveity from Carryan, County Fermanagh owned a cow that gave birth to ten calves in four years in the following manner: two the first year, three the second, two the third and three the fourth. All were healthy heifer calves and lived. McAveity grew rich, till he sold the cow.

∽

A RARE 17th-century coin found in a box of brass weights over 20 years ago fetched a staggering €75,760 at auction in London in September 2005. The Duke of Ormonde pistole, with a face value of 13 shillings and 4 pence, was bought by a private collector after being put up for sale by the lucky finder at coin and medal specialists Dix Noonan Webb. The coin was struck in 1646/47 when James Butler, Duke of Ormonde, Lord Lieutenant of Ireland and Lieutenant-General of the king's forces in Ireland, feared the defection of his troops unless the Royalist garrison in Dublin was paid. Only ten other pistoles are known to have survived from the period, seven of which are owned by the National Museum of Ireland.

∽

WHEN Dubliner Andrew Shannon bought an old padlock for €10 from a market stall in Athy, County Kildare in

2002, he had no idea what a bargain he had actually got. It was only a few years later that his lucky find proved its worth. For several years he stored the ornate and beautiful antique padlock in a cupboard in his Bride Street flat with other curios he had collected, and had given it little thought since.

After a car accident, followed by four heart attacks, 40-year-old Andrew decided to sell all his curios. He showed the padlock to a Sotheby's expert in Dublin, who valued the ancient-looking lock at between €2,000 and €2,500. The etched padlock turned out to have been made in southern Germany in 1556. The rectangular-shaped lock comprised a pair of tubular interlocking arms secured by a series of internal loops and sprung bolts and fitted with a handle on each side, is inscribed with the date and the initials HS. The coats of arms on it are those of the Gugel of Nuremberg, created Barons of the Holy Roman Empire in 1543, and Saurzapfen, Knights of Bavaria.

Andrew was delighted and had it auctioned by a specialist London antique arms and armour auctioneer, Thomas del Mar, in mid-December 2005. It was sold for the stunning figure of just under €60,000 to a private collector. This incredible price was a world record for a lock and many times the pre-sale estimate. Its Dublin vendor knew that it was special when he first saw it, but had no idea it would prove to be a once-in-a-lifetime find. Shannon said, 'It had no key and when I asked the lady how much she wanted she said: "Give me a tenner." I paid up and as I was walking away she called me back to say she had found the key. I was amazed. I put the square-shaped key in the lock and it fitted perfectly, but I only learned how to open it six months ago. I was watching television and saw a lock like it and so I began fiddling with the mechanism and suddenly it sprang open. It works perfectly for something 450 years old.'

❦

DAVID Gallaher (1868–1917) from Ramelton, County Donegal captained the first New Zealand All Blacks Rugby Team for their tour in Europe in 1905/06. His family had emigrated to New Zealand in search of a better life when Gallaher was just five years old. The Donegal man is still revered as a hero in his adopted country. During their visit to Ireland in 2005, the All Blacks rugby team paid a visit to the small Donegal town to attend the unveiling of a plaque at Gallaher's birthplace. He was killed in Flanders in 1917. Earlier in 2005, the All Blacks team had visited his grave in Belgium in an emotional pilgrimage.

❦

IN 1773, a County Carlow labourer discovered a frog with two heads and eight legs while he was cutting a field of wheat.

❦

IS 62-year-old Tipperary-born Mrs Annie O'Brien Ireland's youngest ever great-grandmother? On 9 November 1959 she was pictured with her daughter, Mrs Jean Curley, and Mrs Curley's daughter, Mrs Anne Ivers of Mornington, Drogheda, and Mrs Ivers's newborn baby girl, Anne.

∽

AN account of what must be the strangest operation in Irish medical history is faithfully recorded in the *Dublin Journal of Medical Sciences* of 1843. Under the title 'Transplanting a sheep's tooth into the jaw of a child', this bizarre procedure is described in some detail.

In 1841, Mr Twiss of County Kerry extracted a broken front tooth from a young lady, aged 12 years, and put in its place the front tooth of a yearling sheep, having shortened its root by a quarter of an inch. After the first week, the tooth, initially being much too small for the space, became more and more firm, and had enlarged, but not so much as it would have done in its pristine state, a circumstance observed in transplanting trees. Mr Twiss selected the sheep because of the extreme cleanliness of that animal and the beauty and aptitude of the teeth at two or three years old, when they are about the size of adult human teeth and more likely to grow when transplanted. The root may be shortened or pared to fit and kept in situ by waxed silk ligatures.

∽

A LIBERAL-minded Dublin cat raised two young orphan rabbits alongside her own kitten. A wonderful photograph of this unlikely family is in the *Irish Independent* of 12 May 1934.

∽

MONSIGNOR James J. Dunne (1859–1934), who was parish priest of Donnybrook, Dublin, knew the Bible by heart in Latin and English. He could recite chapters and entire books without a pause.

⁂

WHEN aged 118, Owen Duffy had a youngest son aged two and an oldest son aged 90. He lived near Monaghan town and died in the 1850s.

⁂

ON 29 May 1911, a County Cavan cow swallowed a watch which kept on ticking. Under the headline of 'Watch Ticked in Cow', *The Anglo-Celt* newspaper of 3 June featured this remarkable story on its front page. When a labourer who was working in Garryduff bog, three miles from Ballybay, returned to his work after his midday meal, he discovered that his coat had been torn to shreds by a curious cow. She had swallowed pieces of the coat along with his watch, which was in a pocket. A veterinary surgeon examined the cow the following day and declared that he could hear the watch ticking inside the animal. The cow suffered no ill-effects from its strange diet.

⁂

IRISH-born Captain Edward England plied his trade on the high seas in the early decades of the 18th century and earned a reputation as a moderately successful pirate. After his crew mutinied and put him ashore on Mauritius in the Indian Ocean, England made his way by sea to the notorious pirate haunt of Madagascar, where he died in poverty in 1721. The captain may not have cut much of a dash as a pirate, but he left an enduring legacy all the same. The Jolly Roger – a white skull above crossed bones on a black background – was England's invention.

⚓

AFTER he had earned his degree in medicine in 1827, Dublin-born Dr John Coulter (c.1800–62) immediately joined a whaling ship heading for the exotic South Seas in search of adventure and found more than he had bargained for. Over the next few years, he had many strange encounters and adventures. He was once captured by the warlike natives of the Marquesas Islands in the south Pacific and was left with no choice but to be tattooed all over his body. Coulter was lucky that he was able to bargain that his face would remain unmarked. Later he was enlisted to fight in a war against the tribe's enemies. Coulter's shooting skills were much appreciated by his adopted tribe, which was in no hurry to let him go. Eventually he was rescued and made his way home to Dublin, where he settled down and found employment as an obstetrician in the Rotunda

Hospital. Imagine what his patients thought when he rolled up his sleeves for a delivery.

∾

A HOLE in one is an unusual feat in golf, but when it is performed twice on the same course, on the same day and in the same competition, that's news. Playing in the captain's prize competition at Headfort Golf Club, Kells, County Meath on 14 July 1951, Herbert Tease and Garda George Ryan each holed out in one at the eighth hole (132 yards). Garda Ryan went on to win the competition.

∾

SHORTT, Long, Rabbitte and Hare were the names of four Royal Irish Constables stationed in Leimagowra, Kilcar, County Donegal in 1917.

∾

WHAT could rank as the strangest encounter between two Irishmen took place on the island of Papua New Guinea, when Dr John Coulter's ship, the *Hound*, lay at anchor gathering food and water in 1835. Coulter and five other men, armed to the teeth, were exploring the strange countryside when a large, near-naked warrior suddenly appeared. At first the sailors thought it was a native, but then they discovered that this incredible figure was a white man. The striking wild man stepped forward, introduced himself as Terence O'Connell from County Kerry, and shook the men's hands.

O'Connell was an escaped Botany Bay convict who had landed in New Guinea with several other men. All the others had died, but O'Connell had worked his way up the hierarchy of a tribe to become its king. Over the next few days the sailors visited O'Connell's tribal town and even fought alongside his 1,000-strong warrior army against an enemy tribe which had attacked in a vain effort to try and capture the white men. O'Connell led them safely back to the *Hound*'s anchorage and wished them well.

The Kerryman refused to leave his people when offered a free passage back to Ireland because he had sworn to his people to live out his days with them in the jungles of New Guinea. After a tearful goodbye, Coulter and his fellow sailors watched him disappear once more into the trees. Back home in Dublin, John Coulter published his unique experiences in two highly entertaining books (in 1845 and 1847), packed with adventure and sensational descriptions of encounters with savages.

❧

A FORTUNE that came too late was revealed by the death of a poor 71-year-old Irishwoman in later October 1931, when Miss Minnie Gommon was found dead in a small room she had occupied for many years in the Paris suburb of Courbevoie. Miss Gommon had not been seen for almost a week when the concierge got suspicious and notified the police. They broke into her room and found her dead, apparently from a heart attack. On the floor of her room lay an unopened letter from her Paris lawyer, telling her that she had inherited £8,000. Little was actually known about Miss Gommon other than that she had been employed by a well-known Paris dressmaker for over 30 years, but had retired some years earlier.

❧

FOR many years, the world's largest rope factory was the Belfast Ropework Company. At its peak in the 1930s, it employed 40,000 people and produced over 20,000 tons of rope a year.

∽

A REMARKABLE mirage was witnessed by the people of Devlin, Louisburgh, County Mayo in early August 1948. Looking out to sea, they were startled to see a strange island where there was not even a rock. They saw what appeared to be men moving about it with white coats with rods and guns in their hands. The men they saw seemed to be getting into boats. One man saw it first and called other villagers out to verify what he could see. The old people of the village said that a similar sight had appeared in the ocean about 70 years before.

∽

IN 1888, Gun Wa – in reality a brilliant Irish conman named William H. Hale, who was masquerading as a Chinese physician – arrived in Denver, Colorado and established the Gun Wa Herb Remedy Company, selling 'medicine' that claimed to be able to cure every medical illness under the sun, from baldness to cancer. One story says that Hale himself played the part of a Chinese man during 'consultations' with clients, while another indicates that he may have hired a Chinaman to portray Gun Wa. What is not in question is that Hale was a clever salesman and thrived for a few years by selling his spurious wares. But when he tried to establish a mail order business, he was charged with misrepresenting his product and ended up in court. Hale was also indicted for mailing pornographic materials. He was no fool and fled to England before he could be convicted on either charge.

Stupidly, he went back to the United States a few years later, thinking he was safe. Hale was arrested, convicted of mail fraud and sent to a federal prison in Joliet, Illinois for a year. The colourful Irish conman was last heard of in 1916, when he was thought to have been working a medical scam in Mexico.

∽

THE world's first hydro-powered train and the first electrified railway in Ireland or Britain ran from Portrush to Bushmills village in County Antrim between 1882 and 1949 (in 1887 it was extended a further 3 km to the magnificent Giant's Causeway). Powered by a small generating station at the nearby Salmon Leap waterfall, this train was a considerable asset to local tourism. It was designed by local-born engineer William Traill (1844–1933). Trail also invented the third conducting rail system (which supplied the power), still used by many underground railways.

∽

AN amusing incident occurred in the first round of the Senior Hurling Championship played at Galway on a Sunday in early May 1938 between Claregalway and Galway City. Several players from each team wore new hurling boots and the game had not long started when one of the players, finding that wearing his unbroken-in new boots was too painful, sat down and took them off. He continued to play in his stockinged feet. Other players followed his example and before half-time at least 15 of the 30 players had removed their boots.

∽

ONE of the most bizarre church memorials is that of the great Donegal-born 18th-century actor Charles Macklin (c.1690–1797) in St Paul's Church in Covent Garden, London. He designed his own memorial, to remind others that he had once killed a man. Macklin was notoriously hot-tempered and was always getting into arguments and fights – usually with his fellow actors. In 1735, Macklin accidentally killed another actor during an argument over a wig. In a fit of rage, Macklin lunged at the man with his cane. It went through the man's eye and he died. A remorseful Macklin pleaded self-defence at the trial that followed and escaped hanging, but he never forgot the terrible fight. When he died in 1797, Macklin left instructions that a memorial showing a skull pierced by a knife should be placed above his grave. It can still be seen on the wall of St Paul's.

∽

AT the weekly meeting of the Clare GAA County Board in early July 1931, an unusual point arose in relation to the recent Clooney–Crusheen hurling match, which Crusheen had won by a point. The Clooney club asked for a replay on the grounds that a ball which was going over the dead ball-line had been stopped by a dog – presumably a Crusheen supporter – and a goal was scored as a result. The Crusheen delegate saw 'no sense at all' in the statement, but the County Board took it seriously enough to adjourn the question, pending the referee's official report on the incident. A delegate humorously asked if beagles were being trained to follow the interests of their owners on the hurling field.

❦

MICHAEL Bradley of Ballinasloe, County Galway made a model church in four months in 1957/58 – using 100,000 matchsticks. It was fitted with electric lights and the interior had pews and tiny statues.

❦

CHILDHOOD friends who had not seen each other for 20 years encountered each other again in strange circumstances during Ireland's worst-ever motorway pile-up on the M7 in County Kildare on 27 March 2007. Patrick Dowling became trapped in his car after an overturned cement truck pulverised it. William Gilchrist was driving behind Mr Dowling and witnessed the accident. 'I saw the cement lorry overturn directly on top of someone's car in front of me,' he recalled. 'It completely crushed it. The car was like a pancake. I was afraid to look into the wreck. When I did, I saw only the driver's seat wasn't touched. Then I saw Patrick. I've been living in America these past 15 years and I've been home less than a year, but I recognised Patrick from school. He was completely unscathed. It was a miracle.' William dragged his long-lost and extremely lucky friend to safety.

❦

SKILFUL use of the *Oxford English Dictionary* by two appellants in a court case saved them a fine on 4 April

1978. 'A pale is definitely not a pole,' Eamonn Farrell successfully argued in the Circuit Court. He hammered home his point by quoting the *OED* definition. He convinced the judge and won his case. It was an unusual case, where two men from Ballymun were appealing against a District Court conviction on a charge of sticking posters on a lamp-post. They had been fined £2 each. Eamonn O'Farrell and Joe Davis, both of the Socialist Party, argued that there was nothing illegal about sticking their posters on lamp-posts, and O'Farrell referred to the 1842 Police Act. It stated that it was illegal to post signs on a building, wall, fence or pale owned by somebody else, 'but nowhere does it say anything about a lamp-post,' he emphasised. Judge Buchanan agreed with the appellants and overturned the conviction. 'Under the Act, a pale is not a pole,' he admitted.

❧

THE first recorded visit of a Madeiran fork-tailed petrel (*Oceanodroma castro*) to Ireland ended quite quickly when it hit the lantern of the Blackrock, County Mayo lighthouse on 18 October 1931. The assistant light-keeper there, D.J. O'Sullivan, recognised it as an unusual species and sent the bird's carcass to the Natural History Museum in Dublin.

The unfortunate bird was certainly a long way from home. Its natural habitat was the Azores and Madeira islands off the west coast of Africa. It was the first known visit of this species in Ireland. Three other birds had previously been sighted in Britain.

❧

DUBLINER Hilda Costello died twice but lived to tell

the tale. The first 'death' occurred in 1951 when she had to have an emergency operation. She was 'dead' for seven minutes. The second happened in September 1957 during one of her quarterly medical checks. That time, her 'death' lasted for nearly 20 minutes. At the time, a doctor said that nearly 12 people annually 'died' that way, but it was highly unusual for a person to die twice this way – and live to talk about it.

≺

IN January 1958, 19-year-old Hanna Jorgenson from Glendalough, County Wicklow (originally from Jutland in Denmark) became the first non-Irish person to be employed as an airhostess with Aer Lingus. She spoke Irish, English, French and all the Scandinavian languages. Hanna had come to Ireland with her parents and brothers when she was ten.

≺

DR William Harvey relates an extraordinary case, which he learned from George Carew, Earl of Totnes and Lord-Lieutenant of Munster, of a hardy, heavily pregnant woman who followed her soldier husband as the army marched to Kinsale in 1601. On the march the army halted for an hour near a small river. Feeling that she was going to go into labour soon, the woman retired to a thicket and gave birth to twins without any assistance. After she had washed them and herself in the river, she wrapped the infants in a blanket and tied them to her back. The same day, she marched barefoot 12 miles with the army without any complaint and appeared to be none the worse for her experience. The next day, Carew and the Viceroy, Charles Blount, Earl Mountjoy (who was leading the army), were so impressed with the mother's toughness that they acted as the infants' godfathers and were delighted when the two boys were given their Christian names, George and Charles. Harvey's account of this woman can be found in *The Works of William Harvey* (1847).

≪

KATHERINE Fitzgerald (1660–1725) was the heiress to the large estate of Dromana Castle, County Waterford. After her parents' deaths, her uncle, Lord Power of Curraghmore, became her guardian, but he was an ambitious and unscrupulous man who coveted her inheritance and abused his position of trust. He planned to add the Dromana estate to his family's by marrying Katherine to his son and heir, John. In 1673, no less a personage than the Archbishop of Canterbury officiated at the cousin's wedding in his chapel at Lambeth Palace, even though she was only twelve and a half and her bridegroom was not yet eight years of age.

Three years later, Katherine rebelled against her fate and appealed to the archbishop for an annulment on the grounds that she had never consented to the arranged marriage. She had fallen in love with a dashing young officer called Edward Villiers and was not going to be denied her true love. Katherine eloped and married Edward Villiers. It was fortunate her new husband was well connected: another member of his family, Barbara Villiers, Duchess of Cleveland, was a favourite mistress of King Charles II. No doubt her influence helped the lovers' cause. A long legal battle to establish the validity of her marriage followed, but Katherine and Edward ultimately triumphed and her uncle's scheming came to nothing.

᪥

BELFAST-born Henry Joy McCracken (1767–98) was a United Irishman active in the 1798 Rebellion. He was hanged at the old market-house in Belfast – on ground that had been given to the town by his great-great-grandfather – opposite the house on Rosemary Street where he himself was born.

᪥

LITTLE is known about Mary McMullen's background (other than the fact that she was Irish), but she became famous in the 1820s for her incredible long-distance walking performances in England, earning her the moniker 'the Female Pedestrian'. She travelled from town to town undertaking these walks for money (often in far-from-ideal conditions). It is thought that her career was not particularly lucrative, so she 'walked' regularly in front of large crowds – the largest recorded being 6,000 strong – and was none the worse for it.

Her heyday was probably one ten-week period towards the end of 1826 (when she was about 62 years of age) when she completed five marathon walks (three of 92 miles, one of 40 miles and another of 20 miles). She did two of these longer walks inside four days. It is likely that many of her performances have gone unrecorded. Despite the many unplanned interruptions and breaks to eat, drink and rest, Mrs McMullen could cover 20 miles inside four hours, 40 miles inside nine, and 92 miles within 24 hours.

She is described as a tall woman who wore a long dark skirt, white cotton blouse, coloured scarf, white muslin cap and black stockings. Mrs McMullen walked in bare feet. Her course was usually a half-mile stretch measured along a public road, on which she walked to and fro. Her way was frequently obstructed by crowds of boys and young men who had bet against her, but she faced them down cheerfully. Her son, Bernard, made his living the same way between 1822 and 1827 and they sometimes travelled together. Those who saw her often remarked on Mary Mc-Mullen's lack of tiredness and the apparent ease with which she performed her remarkable long-distance walks.

∽

LOUGH Achree, Skreen, County Sligo is the youngest natural lake in Ireland. It was formed by an earthquake in 1490.

∽

THE *Hibernian Journal* of 31 March 1788 contains a report of an unusual duel that took place in a field near Drumcondra Road, on the northside of Dublin. Instead of swords or pistols, the protagonists fought with shears, which was a very appropriate choice of weapon considering that both men were tailors. 'There was much sniping at each other,' the newspaper report recounted, 'until a well-directed snip by one of them divided the nostrils of his opponent. But, in a twinkle, the wounded one cut off the right ear of his opponent. Blood thus being drawn on both sides, the seconds interfered, and the rivals were reconciled.'

∽

IN late August 1995, a man staggered into the casualty department of a Belfast Hospital with a wind-up turtle attached to his testicles. He explained to medical staff that his young son had dropped the toy into his bath. 'A mechanical joint connected to his tender bits and jammed solid,' a nurse said.

❦

IN mid-August 1928, John Ryan, a butcher of Emmet Street, Tipperary, gave away a collie dog he had owned for five years. Ryan donated the dog to a friend who lived 20 miles away in Hollyford. Two days later, the butcher came downstairs in the morning to open up his shop and discovered the dog sitting patiently on the doorstep. It had found its own way home overnight and was exhausted.

❦

AN extraordinary freak of nature occurred on the farm of Mount Melleray Monastery, Cappoquin, County Waterford in mid-February 1930. A cow gave birth to a calf which was found to have its heart located in its throat. The calf was over a week old and thriving by the time Irish newspapers reported its existence. The animal was inspected by several veterinary surgeons. There was a noticeable lump in its throat and the regular beating of the heart could clearly be seen through the thin membrane of the neck. Except for remarkable biological misplacement, the calf was just like any other normal calf of its age.

❦

A REMARKABLE mirage was witnessed by several people from Enniskillen, County Fermanagh at 11 p.m. on 26 August 1932. Low down near the western horizon, a striking picture of a broad expanse of water appeared. It was dotted with numerous islands and a stretch of beach on which waves seemed to be beating. The atmosphere was fairly bright, but cloudy. The details of the mirage were very clear and distinct and it lasted for about an hour. It was said that none of the islands depicted bore any resemblance to those in Lough Erne.

❧

IN late April 1932, the *Connacht Tribune* reported that a man from Caherlistrane, County Galway had been hit by lightning and knocked unconscious. After a few hours he woke up, suffering no lasting effects. A similar event took place in the same area on the evening of 2 May 1932, when a heavy thunderstorm broke and a young local man named Patrick Moran was also hit by lightning and knocked unconscious. It took several hours to revive him.

❧

IN the *Lousiville Medical Monthly* of February 1895, Dr Dade describes the case of a 58-year-old Irishwoman who had suffered from an enormous umbilical hernia for over 15 years. It was extremely painful and had progressively increased in size over the years. When Dr Dade examined her, the tumour's circumference measured 19½ inches at the base, 11¼ inches at the extremity and extended 12¾ inches out from the abdominal wall.

A photograph shows how truly shocking the hernia was. The veins covering it were prominent and distended. The circulation of the skin was defective, giving it a blue appearance. Vermicular contractions of the small intestines could be seen at a distance of 10 feet. There was little the doctor could do for the poor woman.

❧

SAUNDERS' News Letter of 4 February 1830 contains a remarkable account of a Dublin body-snatcher who made a living stealing corpses and selling them on to surgeons for dissection in medical colleges. The article was entitled 'A Dutiful Resurrectionist':

'A few nights ago a corpulent midwife named Maginniss, rather aged, died on the north side of the city and on the night of her burial it was discovered that the leader of those who attempted to disinter the poor woman and deliver her body up for dissection was one of her own sons. On the fellow being accused of the crime he said "Sure even if I did so a tenderer hand couldn't go over her".'

❧

THE Museum of the Royal College of Surgeons of Ireland holds a vast range of anatomical specimens and related items. Among its most macabre items is the sketch of a man whose face was eaten away by a pig while he lay in an unconscious drunken state. The incident occurred in 1841. The unfortunate man's entire nose, his cheeks and parts of both ears – in fact, all the edible parts of his face – were chewed off by the animal. All the wounds healed and he recovered, but of course he had great difficulty enunciating, chewing and swallowing as a result of the extensive destruction of the soft parts of his face. Despite his injuries, the man thrived in hospital and adjusted to his new circumstances admirably. His main regret was that he had to forgo his pipe tobacco. The picture shows him after the wounds had all healed, without nose and ears, but with two perfect rows of beautifully white teeth.

❧

A CHERRY stone carved in 1681 by John Clenett, Clonmacken, Sixmilebridge, County Clare clearly showed a horse, a hound, a hare, a stag, a fox, a squirrel, a rabbit and a monkey on one side. On the other side, he carved one of the psalms.

❧

ONE of the strangest weddings on record took place in Dublin on 25 April 1959. Kerry-born Maura Garvey married her fiancé at Harrington Street Church – although he was 5,000 miles away in Venezuela. It was a marriage by proxy. This is rare in the Catholic Church, but Canon Law allows it when restrictions prevent the parties from meeting to marry. Her groom was Declan Gilroy from Dartry, Dublin. He had to leave Ireland four months before the wedding to take up an accountancy position in Venezuela. The unusual ceremony was solemnised by the Rev. Father Foley. The marriage was arranged by ecclesiastical authorities in Ireland and Dublin, because under Venezuelan immigration laws it was impossible for an unmarried woman to enter the country.

❧

THE Museum of the Royal College of Surgeons of Ireland contains a tooth from an Asiatic elephant with a bullet embedded in its centre. The tooth had been penetrated by a hunter's bullet. Afterwards the tooth had closed in over the foreign body as it grew.

❧

AN 18-year-old Irish youth who had served on board the *HMS Mutine* at the Battle of Algiers left Exeter on foot on

18 April 1817, at a quarter past nine in the morning, at the same time as a mail-coach left Exeter, and arrived in Plymouth dock at a quarter to five that afternoon, ahead of the coach. He had covered the 46 miles in seven and a half hours – barefoot.

∽

ONE of the most notorious events in Australian history took place on 19 March 1932, when Dublin-born Captain Francis De Groot (1888–1969) upstaged the New South Wales Premier, Jack Lang, at the official opening of the famous Sydney Harbour Bridge. De Groot had served in the 15th Hussars on the western front in World War I, where he was awarded a ceremonial sword. After the war he moved to Australia and went into business as an antiques dealer and furniture manufacturer. He also joined a right-wing paramilitary organisation called the New Guard, which was strongly opposed to the left-wing government of the time. When the leader of the New Guard publicly swore that Lang would not open the bridge, the authorities were put on high alert at the ceremony.

Captain De Groot made a mockery of security arrangements when he showed up uninvited on horseback in his military uniform and blended in with other soldiers on horseback guarding the dignitaries. Premier Lang was about to cut the ribbon to formally open the bridge when De Groot rode forward, drew his ceremonial sword and, reaching down from his mount, flamboyantly slashed the ribbon, declaring the bridge open 'in the name of the decent and respectable people of New South Wales'. He said this was in protest because the Governor General of Australia, Sir Isaac Isaacs, had not been invited to perform the ceremony. De Groot was arrested and his sword confiscated.

De Groot had carefully planned his actions and ensured that all were legal, which was highly embarrassing for the authorities – just as he had calculated. All they could do was charge him $5 for trespassing. De Groot was not finished yet. He sued for wrongful arrest on the grounds that a police officer had no right to arrest an officer of the Hussars. An out-of-court settlement was reached and De Groot's beloved sword was returned to him. He later came back to Ireland, where he died. In 2004 his family sold the sword and it was purchased by a company in Australia which gave tours of the Sydney Harbour Bridge. Dramatic film footage exists of De Groot opening the bridge in 1932.

⋘

NICOLE Carolan's family were delighted when she was born at Cavan Hospital on 12 February 2007. Amazingly, her mother and grandmother share the same birthday. Her mother, Marian, was born on 12 February 1974 and her grandmother, Bernadette Gorman, was born on that day in 1949.

⋘

THE lighthouse keepers of Tuskar Rock off the coast of County Wexford performed heroically during a blizzard at the end of February 1933. They struggled to keep the lantern clear of snow. During the night, the persistently heavy snowfall looked as if it would completely cover the glass sides of the lantern. If this had occurred, the beacon would have been obscured, with serious consequences for shipping. Realising this, the brave keepers, armed with mops saturated in paraffin, ventured onto the tiny balcony around the top of the lighthouse, over a hundred feet above the boiling sea.

They cleared the accumulated snow from the glass and rubbed the paraffin all over it so that the snow would thaw immediately on coming into contact with the oil. This dangerous operation had to be performed several times throughout the night.

There was another hazard to contend with. Hundreds of starlings, blown out to sea in the blizzard, were attracted by the brilliant light. Huge numbers of them flew against the thick glass of the lantern and were killed. In the morning, hundreds of the birds, dead and dying, littered the rock at the base of the tower.

～ふ

IN April 1993, Seán McGovern from The Neale, County Mayo caught a 3½ lb pike while fishing on Lough Mask. When he landed the specimen fish, he discovered that it had a 3½ lb trout in its mouth.

～ふ

THE last public execution in Ireland took place at the front of Downpatrick prison when John Logue from Ballymachrennan, County Down was hanged for shooting a ten-year-old boy to death.

The last woman to be publicly executed in Ireland was Honorah Stackpole from Swallow Bridge, County Clare. She was hanged outside Ennis prison on 29 April 1853. With three relatives, she had conspired in the death of a rich cousin. They were also caught and hanged in Ennis on the same day as Honorah.

⌘

A FREAK potato which formed a perfect shamrock shape went on display in a shop window in Northgate Street, Athenry, County Galway in November 1923.

⌘

FLORENCE Court House in County Fermanagh contains several curious items. When William Cole, 2nd Earl of Enniskillen, returned from a grand tour of Europe as a young man, he brought back a most unusual table. It is made from the lava of Mount Vesuvius and is one of only six of its kind in the world. Elsewhere in this stately home is a mounted hoof from Sulky, one of six horses from which the bloodline of all thoroughbreds is derived.

⌘

SOME years ago, Rommel the dachshund, owned by the Montgomery family of Rosemount House, County Down, was badly injured in an accident and left with paralysed back legs. His owners had a special trolley made which could be strapped to Rommel, allowing him to overcome his disability and wheel himself around in comfort.

≪

WHAT must be the first recorded account of a sheep killing a fox took place in County Armagh in January 1994. Protecting her lambs, a 200 lb ewe butted a vixen to death after it had broken into a sheep pen at Hamiltonsbawn, near Richhill.

≪

DUBLIN'S most destructive hailstorm occurred on 17 April 1850. The hailstones were as large as walnuts and broke vast numbers of windows and slates and also crushed crops.

≪

A REMARKABLE feat of endurance was performed on Milltown Golf Course, County Dublin on 24 June 1924. One of the club members, P.K. Love, bet that he could play six rounds of the Milltown links in 100 strokes per round. The Dubliner started early, at 4:30 a.m., and finished that evening at half past eight. With regular breaks for breakfast, lunch and tea, he won his wager with 43 strokes to spare. Love had a different partner for each round and walked close to 20 miles that day.

It was the first time such a feat had been accomplished on an Irish course, but similar performances had previously been achieved by English, Scottish and American golfers on their own golf course.

∽

THE first parishioner to be baptised and the first parishioner to be married in the new church in Kells, County Meath (in 1960), as well as the first parishioner to be buried from it, bore the same surname – Smith.

∽

ROBERT de Clahull of Offerba was summoned to the Assizes at Clonfert, County Galway, in 1295 to answer for his action in claiming a whale that had been cast up on his land when the country people came from near and far to cut it up, as they had done 'since time immemorial'. The prosecution said that 'all great whales of the sea, cast up upon the land, belong to the Crown'. Robert de Clahull pleaded that his father had been granted all 'wrecks of the sea' as often as they washed up on his part of the strand, and that for this privilege he paid six shillings and eight pence a year. The prosecuting council insisted that whales were not wrecks; Robert, in his turn, said that by the ancient laws of Ireland they were. In Irish law, both whales and wrecks were included in this category as 'waifs of the sea'. The case went against de Clahull, who was fined.

৽

THE Australian Hahn Brewing Company had to withdraw advertising for its Irish-style beer in 1994 after a large section of Sydney's Irish community objected to its unusual marketing campaign. Posters advertising the beer featured 'Open other end' on the base of the bottles and the slogan 'It's as Irish as waterproof teabags'. The large Irish population in Australia was not amused.

৽

IT is not uncommon in parts of the world where earthquakes usually occur for small islands to be suddenly engulfed by the sea. Sometimes islands are destroyed by coastal erosion, and at least one Irish island did actually disappear in recent centuries as a result of this slow but unstoppable process. According to several public documents of that period, in the early 1600s the island of Minish in Clew Bay, County Mayo measured some 12 acres. It was surveyed in 1814 and was discovered to have shrunk drastically over the years and was only 420 feet long and 30 feet wide. Two years later, it disappeared altogether.

৽

THE September 1791 issue of *Country Magazine* carries a report of a four-year-old boy who was carried off and killed by an eagle in Clonmenny, County Donegal.

৽

IN October 1843, Cobh (then called Cove) had a narrow escape from destruction by bombardment. *HMS Lynx*, a vessel mounting three guns, was lying out in the harbour when her commander, Captain Burslem, gave the order to clear the decks for action. The order was quickly obeyed and the three guns were primed and loaded while the crew waited in breathless silence for what was to follow. The ship's officers were horror-struck on hearing the order and, though they fully realised the risk of interfering with a command given by their captain, they felt justified in preventing it from being carried out in view of the almost certain loss of life and property that would inevitably follow.

A consultation between the officers was held and it was decided to countermand the order. The captain was induced to go to his cabin and suspend the order. The matter was then reported to the Admiralty. Captain Burslem was removed and the *Lynx* proceeded to the Shannon under the command of her First Lieutenant. A report in *The Southern Reporter* that month stated that Captain Burslem had showed signs of 'impaired intellect' on two or three previous occasions, but never to such an extent.

෴

'PASS If You Can' was the name of an inn in Ballymun, County Dublin during the 18th century.

෴

IS this the longest Irish surname? It is inscribed on a vault near Shane's Castle, County Antrim. It reads: 'This vault was built by Shane MacBrien MacPhelim MacShane MacBrien MacPhelim O'Neill esquire in the year 1722.'

෴

WHEN she reached her 106th birthday in January 1906, hale and hearty centenarian Kate Martin of Lislin, near Clones, County Monaghan, danced an Irish jig at her birthday party at a neighbour's house.

࿇

BY a strange coincidence, three past pupils of St Ignatius College, Galway were accidentally reunited after last seeing each other over a quarter of a century earlier. The bizarre meeting took place at the headquarters of the *Irish Independent* newspaper in Dublin on 21 April 1934. The first Galway man, who had spent the previous 26 years living in Buenos Aires, dropped into Independent House to buy a copy of the Eucharistic Congress Souvenir of June 1932.

His entry was synchronised with that of a suntanned stranger back from India after a quarter of a century. The men instantly recognised each other as former classmates. A short while later, another classmate arrived at the offices. The trio had not met for over 27 years.

࿇

KILKENNY-born revolutionary James Stephens (1824–1901) was one of the founders of the Fenian movement. As a result of his activities, he spent many years exiled in Paris. He earned a precarious living through teaching journalism. A little-known fact is that he translated most of Charles Dickens's works into French. At least up until into the 1960s these were still used by the French educational authorities as the standard translations.

࿇

BY March 1958 it was estimated that Herbert Overy of Bray had cycled more than 211,000 miles in the previous 29 years. Each morning he cycled from Bray to Dublin to work as a surgical assistant, then cycled home to Bray in the evening. You might think that he went through many bicycles. In fact, he had used only two, and the one he was riding in 1958 had been in use for 20 years.

❧

TEN-year-old Ross Behan was dead for 20 minutes before being brought back to life. Ross had been underwater for 10 minutes before firemen rescued him from the bottom of the Grand Canal, near Dolphin's Barn, Dublin, on 6 April 2007.

His heart had stopped beating by the time he was dragged from the water, but fireman Andy O'Connor kept administering heart massage to the unresponsive boy as he was rushed to Our Lady's Hospital for Sick Children in Crumlin. Doctors worked on Ross for 20 minutes when he had no heartbeat. Amazingly, he survived the ordeal and has made a complete recovery.

❧

JAMES Reid from Belfast emigrated to America in the mid-19th century and went into business as a gunsmith in New York. His most famous firearm is the aptly named 'My Friend', which he made between 1868 and 1882. This ingenious weapon was a .41 calibre seven-shot pistol-knuckleduster combination. It was favoured by gamblers and women in America for a very good reason: it was small and easily concealable – an ideal weapon for its owner in crowded saloons in frontier towns of the Wild West. Reid later added a short barrel to make the pistol easier to use as a knuckleduster.

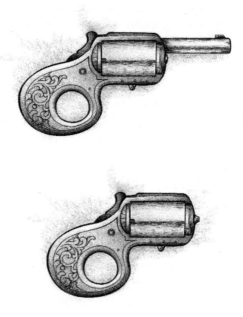

❧

ONLY two copies are extant of the Roll of Honour that contains the names of 50,000 Irishmen who died in World War I. One is in St Patrick's Cathedral, Dublin and the other is in St Columb's Cathedral, Derry. These 10 volumes list each soldier by name, rank and age.

❧

THE 12 animal-strong giraffe herd at Fota Wildlife Park, County Cork is the largest in Britain or Ireland.

※

FOURTEEN-year-old Dublin girl Pauline Mortimer set a new world teeth-cleaning marathon record on 22 August 1981 when she cleaned her teeth continuously for 8 hours 30 minutes at her home.

※

ON 19 December 2006, 618 children gathered at St Oliver's National School, Killarney, County Kerry and created a new world record for the greatest number of people participating in a Secret Santa event. The record was verified by the *Guinness Book of Records*. Secret Santa, or Kris Kindle, is the long-established tradition where people group together to buy one another Christmas presents.

※

THE eight sons and two daughters of Dr William and Beryl Waldron of Knocknacarra, County Galway all qualified as doctors from University College, Galway between 1976 and 1990. According to the *Guinness Book of Records*, this is a world record for the most doctors in one family.

※

EIGHTEEN-year-old Anne Keane from Kilkee, County Clare accidentally took a very roundabout route to Manchester on 21 August 1995. She arrived at Shannon Airport three hours early for her British Airways flight. Her luggage was put on the plane but was taken off when she failed to board after a series of loudspeaker announ cements. The flight left without her. Afterwards, an airport official directed her to the Belavia flight for Minsk, which took off from the same pier. The unfortunate Clare woman landed in the Belarus capital with no passport or visa and was thrown into jail for the night. Anne was freed after a Lufthansa official arranged a free flight to Frankfurt, Germany. British Airways flew her the rest of the way to Manchester free of charge. Thirty-four hours after leaving her home in Kilkee, she arrived at her intended destination.

❧

WHEN his second wife's beloved pet dog died in 1804, Clotworthy Skeffington, 2nd Earl of Massereene, of Antrim Castle, had the animal buried in the grounds in a specially constructed coffin. The eccentric peer gave orders that '50 dogs should attend the funeral in white scarfs and all the dogs of the parish should be present'.

❧

ONE of the most unusual buildings in Ireland was the Bone House at Caledon, County Tyrone. This bizarre structure once served as a summerhouse and had a front constructed entirely of bones. In was built in the 1740s by John Boyle, 5th Earl of Orrery, who was a keen gardener. The building was rectangular, with a large bay to the rear. To the front, five large pillars were formed by setting thousands of femurs and similar long cattle bones directly into lime mortar. The bones were laid in regular courses with the knuckles outwards. Though now in ruins, its remaining 'ivory' pillars glinting in the sun give some idea of how startling the building must have been in its prime.

❧

ANNE Jane Thornton (1818–77) from Ballyshannon, County Donegal fell in love with a young American sea captain called Alexander Burke. When he was suddenly called back to America, she disguised herself and followed him there, working as a cabin-boy under the name of Jim Thornton. When Anne Jane reached New York, she found that her lover had died from cholera. She decided to return to Ireland. Still disguised as a boy, she worked on several ships for the next 31 months. It was not until she joined the *Sarah* (bound for London), commanded by Belfast man Captain John MacEntyre, that she came anywhere near Ireland.

Her secret became public knowledge in February 1835 when a customs officer in the Port of London discovered that 'young Jim' was actually a girl. Overnight she became famous and received many proposals of marriage. She was offered the huge sum of £500 to appear on stage, but the young Donegal woman wanted only to go home to her family. A huge crowd gathered in Donegal Town to greet the adventurous woman on her arrival. King William IV awarded her a generous pension of £10 a year. Another benefactor bought out the lease of a farm her family had previously rented and gave it to her. A year after being re-united with her family, Anne Jane Thornton was a rich young woman, but her problems were far from over.

In February 1836 her boyfriend (from Ballyshannon) paid a visit to see her in Donegal Town and found her held captive by a crowd of men who were dragging her off to church to be married to one of them so that he (and they) could gain possession of her fortune. Her boyfriend rescued her and they were married the next day. That November, she gave birth to a son, whom she named William in honour of the kind king. After that, the adventurous Donegal woman slipped into obscurity. Perhaps her descendants are still around?

෧

ON 15 June 1895, various fish about 1½ to 2 inches long fell from the skies on the pleasure grounds of Carrigaholt Castle, County Clare at noon on a warm summer's day. Some men were working in the gardens when they fell. The castle's owner, W.C.V. Burton, wrote a detailed account and sent specimens of the fish to leading newspapers as evidence of the unusual event. He preserved a large specimen in spirits as a souvenir. Ireland is no stranger to such unusual occurrences. The *Annals of the Four Masters* says that a shower of fish fell in Tirconnell, County Donegal in 1566. In a footnote to this entry, the 19th-century scholar John O'Donovan (who edited the book for publication in 1856) added that a shower of herrings had fallen out of the sky near Slievemore, on Achill Island off the County Mayo coast, in the 1830s. The fish lay putrid on the fields for some weeks afterwards.

෧

DUBLN-born Alexander Mitchell (1780–1868) became blind in his early twenties as a result of childhood smallpox, but that did not hinder his career as a successful inventor. Mitchell's most notable creation was his underwater screw-pile system, which he patented in 1833. Before then, it had not been possible to erect a lighthouse structure in sandy areas. Mitchell devised a system using threaded cast-irons up to a foot wide, which could be firmly screwed into soft or sandy ground to secure the structure. His system was widely used to build lighthouses around the world.

∾

ELLEN McCann, Cloghog, Stewartstown, County Tyrone, died in 1889 aged 104 years. Shortly before her death, she sent her 80-year-old son to transact some business at Stewartstown fair. Hearing that he was drinking in a pub, the sprightly centenarian went into the premises, beat him with a stick and sent him home.

∾

SAMUEL Bisset (1721–83) from Perth, Scotland has a special place in the annals of show business. He was the first man to train a pig for the stage and his prize student was one from Belfast. The remarkable animal trainer settled there in 1775 after a highly successful tour of Britain and Ireland with his menagerie of specially trained animal acts. Early in 1782, Bisset purchased a black piglet from Belfast Market for three shillings. He spent nearly two years training the animal to do tricks.

In August 1783, 'The Wonderful Pig' made its debut on stage in Ranelagh, Dublin. Its performance was nothing less than sensational. The pig apparently kneeled, bowed, spelled out names using cardboard letters, told the time, calculated numbers and pointed out the married and unmarried in the audience. Bisset's 'Learned Pig', as it came to be known, was an instant hit with audiences and earned him a considerable amount of money. When Bisset moved his show to another part of the city, he forgot to seek the permission of the local magistrate and a zealous policeman burst on stage and interrupted the show. He destroyed the showman's props and threatened to kill the pig and jail Bisset if they were ever seen in his district again.

The poor Scottish pig trainer never recovered from the shock of this ordeal and died in Newcastle, England a few weeks later, before he had the chance to complete a tour of Britain with his wonderful act. It was left to another man, a Mr Nicholson, to do that and to make his fortune. He bought Bisset's animals and carried on where his unfortunate predecessor had left off. The Learned Pig and its companion acts reached London in February 1785 and was an instant sensation, attracting huge crowds to its performances until its death in November 1788. This wonderful animal was such a celebrity that several newspapers carried its obituary.

∽

THE famous Dublin surgeon Philip Crampton (1777–1858) had such a dread of his body being eaten by rats after his death that, in accordance with his last wishes, his remains were embedded in cement.

∽

THE immense timber roof of Westminster Hall, one of the finest examples of craftsmanship in the world, is made of Irish oak, procured from the site of St Michan's Church, Dublin. The following is the official record of the transaction: 'The fair green or commune, now called Ostomondtowne-greene, was all wood, and hee that diggeth at this day to any depth shall find the grounde full of great roots. From thence, anno 1098, King William Rufus, by licence of Murchard, had that frame of timber, which made up the roofes of Westminster Hall, "where no English spider webbeth or breedeth to this day".'

❧

THE first telegraph cable between Ireland and Britain was laid in 1853 between Donaghadee, County Down and Portpatrick in Scotland.

❧

ELEVEN one-armed players opposed 11 one-legged players in a cricket match in Derry in 1845. The one-armed side won by 39 runs.

❧

BEFORE March 1962, parcels had to be stamped individually by staff in Dublin's General Post Office. Although there was a machine that could frank letters in bulk, magazines and parcels still had to be processed laboriously by hand until a clever Dublin man, Brendan Scally from Santry, invented a machine that could frank them at a rate of 300 a minute, compared to the manual rate of about 30 to 35 parcels a minute. Scally spent two years designing his machine, which could deal with a wide variety of parcels, stamping them at a constant speed. According to a newspaper of the period, Scally had applied for a patent and had received inquiries from around the world about his ingenious machine.

❧

AFTER the greyhounds Lord Drogheda and Terry finished neck-and-neck at Shelbourne Park, Dublin on 22 July

1918, the race was re-run. They finished in a dead heat again. The race was re-run for a third time with, astonishingly, the same result.

❧

GARDAÍ and soldiers in Waterford city were baffled by the overnight appearance of seven mystery tubular frames attached to parachutes in different parts of the city on 5 October 1998. Each object consisted of an orange and white parachute attached to a heavy aluminium tubular frame about a metre square. It took two men to carry each frame. A test tube was fixed in the centre of the frame. Each one was filled with sand or soil, topped by a blue, inky substance and a clear liquid. The test tubes were sealed with wax to keep the contents intact. Initially it was assumed that the objects had been dropped from a plane, but nobody had seen them land.

Once they were discovered, gardaí called in the Army Bomb Disposal Unit, which quickly established that the frames posed no danger. At first it was thought that they were part of a scientific experiment and were Russian in origin because there were was Cyrillic script on the parachutes. Both the Irish and the British meteorological offices denied carrying out any experiments in the area and had no know-ledge of the device.

No one was any wiser about their origin – even after worldwide media attention. Two days later, Paul Gregg, an American artist living in Waterford, admitted that he had placed the objects around the city in the early hours of 5 October with the help of some friends.

෴

KENNETH Crooks from Cookstown, County Tyrone hooked the biggest catch of his life on 6 February 1999, exactly a year after his previous largest catch and at exactly the same location. He caught the monster pike of 29 lb 11 oz (6 lb more than his previous best) at Lough Gara, County Roscommon. On both occasions, Crooks was fishing with his friend Peter O'Neill – and the two catches were witnessed by Lough Gara regular Alastair Rawlings.

෴

CHRISTMAS came early in November 2005 for Irish prawn fishermen from Kilkeel in County Down and Clogherhead in County Louth when they accidentally netted gift packs of Carolan's Irish Cream Liqueur along with their usual catch. Each pack contained a bottle and two glasses. Around 8,000 of the packs, worth close to £128,000 sterling, had been lost during storms in the Bay of Biscay the month before, en route to Spain for the Christmas market. While fishing in an area off the coast of England known as 'The Smalls', they made their astonishing haul. The liqueur gift packs were perfectly preserved, despite spending nearly a month in the sea.

❧

BARNEY and Mona Foster of Enfield, County Meath had three children who shared the same birthday: David, born 26 March 1955, Helen, born 26 March 1957, and Linda, born 26 March 1959. The likelihood of this occurence is said to be one in 50,000,000.

❧

FERMANAGH-born hell-raiser Bryan Maguire (c.1780–1835) is said to have had his wife help him with his target practice. She held a lighted candle at arm's length for him to aim at. Presumably he was an excellent shot.

Harry Dyas, a famous horse trainer from Boltown Hall, Kilskyre, County Meath, favoured a more extreme form of target practice. Dyas was famed as a crack shot and sometimes practised 'William Tell'-style in a manner that would earn jail in modern times. In the 1930 book *Triumph and Tragedies of the Turf*, his brother-in-law, Campbell Russell, describes how Dyas often placed an apple or egg on the head of a stable boy and would blow it to pieces with a shot from a rook rifle at a distance of 40 yards. The stable boys were said to have had total confidence in Dyas's aim. Indeed, Dyas had an international reputation as an excellent shot and competed abroad with distinction.

❧

AN escaped parrot turned himself in at Buncrana garda station on 3 November 2006 after making a dash for freedom from his home a mile away. His owner, Tom Gibson, had spent the night worrying about how Charlie would cope outside in the freezing night, but the two-year-old African Grey parrot turned up unharmed at the local garda station. Garda Alistair Lee was enjoying a cup of tea when he heard wolf-whistling outside the station. Charlie was 'jailed' in a shed at the back of the station and gardaí contacted local radio stations in order to reunite their unusual prisoner with his owner.

∽

IRISH magician John Brenon toured the eastern United States throughout the last decades of the 18th century. His speciality was the Bullet Catch (in his mouth), which he performed while balancing on a high wire. His wife is said to be the first female magician to perform professionally in America (around 1787).

∽

IN June 1946, the *Anglo-Celt* newspaper reported that a woman from Belcoo, County Cavan owned a healthy chicken that had four legs and four wings. A similar freak was reported in the *Southern Star* newspaper in May 1940. The unusual creature was owned by Jack Sexton, Glengarriff Road, Bantry, County Kerry. In May 1946, a chicken with four legs (two on each side of its body) was born on Thessings Poultry Farm in Crookhaven, County Cork. A five-legged chicken was hatched out by a hen owned by Mrs P. Ryan of Rathkiernan, County Kilkenny in May 1944.

∽

IN the *Philosophical Transactions of the Royal Society of London* (vol. LXIV, p. 474), Dr Purcell of Dublin reported that in the summer of 1773 he had carried out an autopsy on the body of a woman who had died (during labour), in the ninth month of pregnancy, in the anatomical theatre of Trinity College, Dublin. On the right side he found a uterus of ordinary size and form, as is usual at this period of gestation. It contained a full-grown foetus, but there was only one ovary attached to a single fallopian tube – there should have been two. On the left side he found a second uterus, unimpregnated and of usual size, to which another ovary and fallopian tube were attached. Both these uteruses were distinct and almost entirely separate. This strange anatomical oddity was later purchased by Dr John Hunter of London for his museum of medical curiosities and was said to have been one of the most valuable specimens in the collection. It may still be there today because the Hunterian Museum is now owned by the Royal College of Surgeons in London. However, during World War II the museum was hit by bombs and a great deal of the collection was destroyed.

∽

COLM Brady of Shallon, Julianstown, County Meath could not complain about the productivity of three of his ewes which lambed in early December 1989. One had triplets, another quads and the third gave birth to six healthy lambs. Coming from a family of 24 himself, Colm was not overawed by the multiple offspring.

∽

A SURPRISE bestseller of 1838 was Corkman Patrick Murphy's *The Weather Almanac on Scientific Principles, showing the State of the Weather for Every Day of the Year 1838* (the book was published in England in late 1837). *Murphy's Almanac*, as it was known, owed its success to an incredible coincidence rather than to its accuracy. January 1838 turned so cold that many rivers (including the Thames) and waterways were frozen over. The coldest day of this wintry, snowy month was 20 January. In the days and weeks that followed, *Murphy's Almanac* became a runaway bestseller entirely because of his entry for 20 January 1838. He had simply written: 'Fair, and probably the lowest degree of winter temperature.'

Murphy became famous overnight; his almanac ran to 45 editions and he made an enormous profit of £3,000. When the 'nine-day' wonder had passed, the sales of *Murphy's Almanac* dwindled because it became obvious that it could not be relied on. According to Brendan MacWilliams in his popular *Irish Times* weather column, 'subsequent analysis suggested that for 1838 as a whole, his predictions were partially right on 168 days, but entirely wrong on the remaining 197 days.'

The Corkman lost his windfall almost immediately on ill-timed speculation and chanced his luck several times over the years, but was never as fortunate again and sales of his almanac were poor. Murphy used to say that if the weather did not turn out according to his predictions in London, it did so elsewhere. He died in 1847. For many years afterwards, the bitter weather of early 1838 was remembered as 'Murphy's winter'.

❧

THE first miner's safety lamp was invented in 1813 by Dr William Clanny (1776–1850) of Bangor, County Down. Until Clanny's invention, miners had used naked candlelight in mines for centuries. This was a risky thing to do because if there was any methane in the air, the flame could ignite it. Explosions were frequent and many lives were needlessly lost. Various people tried to invent a safety lamp for miners, but the ingenious doctor was the first to create a safer form of lighting for colliers. After two years of experimentation, he proudly presented his design to the Royal Philosophical Society in May 1813. It was a lantern-encased oil lamp, isolated from the outside atmosphere by water seals; air was pumped into the lamp through these special seals. Over the next few decades, Clanny designed several improved versions.

∾

AT the age of 105, Kilkenny-born Thomas Shorthall died in 1762 at Landred in Flanders (present-day Belgium). At the siege of Limerick in 1691, he had been an officer in Grace's Regiment. After the Treaty of Limerick was signed, he went to France and enrolled in the French king's army, ultimately attaining the rank of Lieutenant-Colonel. He was wounded at the Battle of Fontenoy and retired a few years later. Upwards of 30,000 people left Ireland after the Treaty of Limerick, and 100,000 followed later. Of all these, the old Kilkenny warrior was the reputed sole survivor of the Wild Geese.

∾

THE 147th anniversary of the birth of the gifted Scottish poet Robert Burns fell on 25 January 1906. By coincidence exactly 147 guests sat down to a dinner given in honour of the poet's anniversary in Dublin that same night.

∾

BRITISH pop singer Lena Fiagbe turned up for the Radio One Roadshow in Bangor, Wales on the right day in July 1994 and wandered around the town confused, because there was no sign of any such event. Meanwhile in Bangor, County Down the live radio party was in full swing. What really annoyed Lena was that she had been in Ireland the previous day and had travelled across to north Wales for her next gig. She missed out on the opportunity to sing her smash hit, 'Got to get it right'.

❧

IN the 1830s, the secluded village of Union Hall, half a mile from Glandore Harbour on the County Cork coast, attracted many sightseers and scientifically minded people from all over Ireland. The object of their interest was regarded by many as a supernatural phenomenon and came to be known as the 'Glandore lights' or 'Harrington's lights', after the person who had caused all the excitement.

A poor labouring man called Thomas Harrington lived in a small cabin close to the seaside, at the foot of Ardagh Hill near Union Hall village. He contracted tuberculosis (then an incurable disease) and lingered, from 1832 to 1838, all the while progressively worsening from this terrible disease. During this time, strange lights were observed from time to time inside the cabin and all over the body of the sick man. News of this strange sight spread far and wide, and many flocked to witness it.

Some saw nothing, while others observed faint glimmerings or brilliant displays of lights flitting from wall to wall in his cabin. The hands of persons held over the body of the sick man sometimes took on a luminous appearance to onlookers in the surrounding darkness. Sceptics thought it a hoax, but could find no evidence. Most folk looked on it as nothing less than a miracle.

The scientifically minded believed that it could be explained by chemical or electrical causes in the atmosphere or the soil the cabin was built on. It was a well-known fact that *Ignis fatuus* (will-o'-the-wisps) were seen at times in boggy, marshy ground or near graveyards and were caused by phosphorous hydrogen escaping from the soil, the result of animal and vegetable decay. On investigation, the soil on and around Harrington's cabin was found to be normal and free-draining.

The cause of this luminosity was finally correctly diagnosed by the man's own doctor, who methodically investigated this phenomenon and discounted all the other theories one by one. Cases like Harrington's were very rare, but recognised by medicine all the same. It had most likely been caused by phosphorous in Harrington oxidising after being released by his slowly decaying body. That is the best interpretation of the diagnosis a layperson can give, but this unfortunate man's condition was written up in many medical journals. The best account is by his own attending physician, Dr Donovan of Skibbereen, and appears in *The Dublin Medical Press* of 15 January 1840.

∞

A FAITHFUL cocker spaniel inadvertently landed its owner on the wrong side of the law in December 1938. When a Mrs J. Kane of Kilglass, Carbery, County Kildare heard shots, she rushed from her house and saw that two of her ducks had been killed. She spotted two persons jumping into a van and driving off. Mrs Kane caught their dog before it could get away with its owners and gave it to

Sergeant Summerville of nearby Edenderry garda station. The sergeant acted quickly and a van fitting the same description was stopped by gardaí as it passed through a neighbouring village.

Its occupants, Joseph Hanlon and his wife, from Dublin, were brought to the garda station. Sergeant Summerville acted on a hunch and released the cocker spaniel when the driver was in the station.

The dog recognised its master immediately and rushed over to Hanlon, licking his hand and acting playfully. Hanlon ignored the dog, so the spaniel ran through the barracks door, jumped into the van and sat down on Mrs Hanlon's lap. Hanlon was fined 40 shillings for 'trespass in pursuit of game' and 40 shillings for carrying a gun.

Mrs Kane was allowed 20 shillings' compensation for the loss of her ducks. The dog was said to be delighted to be reunited with its poorer and wiser owners.

❧

ACCORDING to the *Annual Register* of 1762, honeydew fell 'in the neighbourhood of Rathiermac in Ireland' on 9 July that year. It fell so heavily on trees and grassland that large quantities of it were scooped up and saved.

❧

IN his 1845 book *The Philosophy of Mystery*, Walter Cooper Dendy briefly describes several incredible incidents of sleepwalking. One of these occurred off the east coast of Ireland in 1833. At about two o'clock in the morning, the astonished crew of a coastguard boat picked up a man swimming in the sea. It later emerged that he had left his home about midnight, walked two miles over a dangerous path and had swum about a mile out to sea. After he was taken into the boat, he could not be persuaded that he was not still in his warm bed at home.

∽

THOMAS Lambert was born in May and died in February of the same year! An inscription on a tomb in County Wexford reads: 'The body of Tho., the son of Tho. Lambert, Gent., who was born may ye 13, 1683, and dyed Feb. ye 9 the same year.' This puzzling inscription can be easily explained. Before the Calendar Reform Act in 1752, the first month of the year was March, so that in 1683, February was the last month of the year.

∽

PREMATURE burial was a staple of the press in the 18th and 19th centuries and many examples heightened the public's fear of a hasty interment. One such case from Cork city received widespread media attention at the time. In early June 1815, a soldier of the 93rd regiment, quartered in the city barracks, fell ill and died. After being laid out in the usual way for two days, his corpse was conveyed to the place of interment (St Nicholas's churchyard) on the evening of 6 June. As they lowered the body into the grave, the soldiers heard a struggling noise in the coffin. Opening it, they discovered that the 'corpse' they were in the act of burying was trying to force up the coffin lid with his hands and knees. All were astonished at the turn of events. After a brief moment of shock, the soldiers carried their comrade home in the open coffin.

∽

WHEN London-born bookseller John Dunton visited Malahide, County Dublin in the late 17th century, he noted that the local fishermen trained cormorants to catch fish and return with them to their boats. The birds' necks were ringed to prevent them from swallowing their catches.

᪤

MICHAEL Corrigan from Fermoy, County Cork was one of the most successful conmen operating in London during the 1930s and 1940s. His highly imaginative swindles are legendary. Posing as a general of the Mexican army, he once successfully sold non-existent oil concessions to the British government. On another occasion he played the part of a chief inspector in the Royal Canadian Mounted Police seconded to Scotland Yard and persuaded a West End jeweller to lend him his stock for a day in order to trap a gang of Canadian thieves.

Gullible wealthy American tourists were a favourite target of Corrigan's. He sold the Tower of London, London Bridge (twice), and 145 Piccadilly to them (many times). William Donaldson, who wrote at length about this Cork rogue in his book *Brewer's Rogues, Villains & Eccentrics*, describes him as 'a handsome man of military bearing, and an accomplished actor'.

᪤

ACCORDING to *The Irish Catholic* of 4 August 1988, a gooseberry bush in the garden of Eddie O'Connor of Castleblayney, County Monaghan yielded a crop of blackcurrants. The bush had been left on its own for the whole year and was expected to produce a crop of gooseberries.

A simple explanation is that the bush was a gooseberry–blackcurrant hybrid that occurred naturally. It may also have been a jostaberry bush, which is described as a cross between a blackcurrant and a gooseberry. It was developed in Germany in the 1970s and has been available to the public for some time.

ᢙ

ADOLF Hitler's *Mein Kampf* was first translated into English in 1939 by James Murphy (1880–1946) from Upton, County Cork.

ᢙ

GEORGE Millan of Bangor, County Down carved an incredibly detailed sculpture of Donaghadee Lighthouse from a lump of coal. In 2002 he kindly donated this wonderful object to the Irish Lighthouse Museum at the Baily Lighthouse in Howth.

ᢙ

THE small, rocky island of Inishtrahull off Malin Head, County Donegal is officially the oldest place in Ireland. The rocks there have been dated to be 1,778 million years old. The second-oldest place in Ireland are the rocks at Annagh Head in County Mayo, which are 1,753 million years old.

∽

THE shortest time ever taken to score a hat trick in a football game is 2 minutes 13 seconds by Jimmy O'Connor for Shelbourne against Bohemians at Dalymount Park, Dublin on 19 November 1967.

∽

ON 28 December 2005, a 55-year-old baggage handler at Dublin Airport was accidentally locked into the cargo hold of a transatlantic aeroplane bound for New York. He got stuck in the hold while searching for a misplaced bag and initially did not notice that the plane was taxiing for take-off. Another colleague had closed the cargo-hold door without knowing that his co-worker was inside. It was fortunate that the man had a mobile phone, which he used to phone the base supervisor's officer, who then alerted air traffic control and the plane's pilot. The incident would not have been life-threatening even if the aircraft had taken off because the hold would have been fully pressurised like the passenger cabin and there would have been plenty of oxygen. Some years previously a baggage handler was locked in a hold on a two-hour flight from Philadelphia to Chicago.

∽

CAPTAIN William Stewart was the well-liked commander of the brig *Mary Russell* of Cork – until he murdered seven crewmen during a period of paranoid madness on a voyage back from Barbados in June 1828. Some time after setting sail, the captain began to show signs of strangeness. Convinced his fellow Corkmen were planning to mutiny and take hold of the ship, he decided to act first and slaughter them. He carried out his gruesome plan with cunning subtlety. In order to allay his fears, the unsuspecting crew willingly submitted to being bound hand and foot, thinking that by humouring Stewart they could prevail on him to get some sleep. No sooner had they been rendered powerless than the captain produced a crowbar and beat out their brains in a frenzy of madness.

At his trial in Cork, survivors recounted all the horrific details of the voyage. The captain was found guilty but insane and spent the rest of his life in lunatic asylums in Dublin and Cork. In Cork Lunatic Asylum he laboured for years carefully constructing a model ship out of beef and mutton bones left over from the patients' meals. He was not allowed to use a knife, but this did not deter him. The captain sharpened a bone which he used for carving others. The result was a work of art. From bow to stern along the deck it measured 21 inches. The bones were so finely polished that it looked as if it had been made from ivory. He presented the ship to Dr Thomas Carey Osborne, who was Medical Attendant in the Cork Asylum. Following the doctor's death, Stewart was moved back to Dundrum Asylum in Dublin after killing an attendant during one of his periodic fits of insanity. He died there in August 1873.

⤴

A TOMBSTONE erected in Marmullane Graveyard,
Cork recalls the tragedy:

Timothy Connell, mariner, murdered 1828 on the
Mary Russell out of Cork, by the ship's master.

You gentle reader that do pass this way
Attend a while, adhere to what I say.
By murder vile I was bereft of life
And parted from two lovely babes and wife.
By Captain Stewart I met an early doom
On board the *Mary Russell* the 22nd June.
Forced from the world to meet my God on High
With whom I hope to reign eternally – Amen.

⤴

IN the opening greyhound race on the night of 11 April 1936 at Shelbourne Park, Dublin, the 'hare' stopped at the first bend. In the re-run race, Book Reporter, who was making his first appearance on the track, won easily. The dog was subsequently bought by G.B. Flintham of London. A few weeks later, on 4 May, Book Reporter was given his trial at Wimbledon. The 'hare' stopped at the first bend, and in the re-run race Book Reporter won again easily.

❦

IRELAND'S tallest living man at 7 feet 4 inches, Michael Coulter from Cookstown, County Tyrone, was unable to launch a non-smoking campaign in Northern Ireland schools after he was sentenced to nine months in jail in March 1995 for stealing cigarettes from a petrol station in Lifford, County Donegal. He had other convictions, including a burglary, after which police issued a description of the two suspects to whom they wished to speak. One suspect was about 7 feet 4 inches tall and the other had only one leg.

❦

IN *The Lancet* medical journal of 1863, Dr Bruce mentions the case of a 55-year-old Irishman who, for no apparent reason, suffered from a painful erection for six weeks. It did not subside even when he was chloroformed and rendered unconscious.

❦

BRIAN McMullan of Short Strand, Belfast believes that the life of his one-year-old daughter Ann Marie was saved by his dog's selfless action in September 1996. McMullan's 12-year-old Staffordshire terrier–Labrador cross, Bruno, pounced on a lit firecracker which Ann Marie was about to pick up and swallowed it. The firecracker had been thrown into the McMullan's back garden by youths. It exploded inside Bruno, who lay on his back, trembling. There was blood everywhere and smoke poured from the poor dog's mouth. He was rushed to a vet and treated for a jaw injury.

∞

IN April 1950, Patrick Shortiss of Treacy Park and Patrick Shortiss (no relation) of Lough Street, Carrick-on-Suir admitted being drunk and were given the benefit of the Probation Act. The presiding judge told them, 'You have both the same name – that is a coincidence. Both of you took a drop too much on the same date – another coincidence. Now you are being let off without a fine, and that is another coincidence.'

∞

IRISH leprechauns took a flight to America for St Patrick's Day 1952. A Boeing Stratocruiser took 850 leprechauns from Shannon to New York on 6 March. Of course, they were not real leprechauns – they were plaster models, consigned to the Hibernian Banquet Society in New York for use in the St Patrick's Day festivities.

∞

ENGLISH tourist James Hall recorded that he was vastly amused to see the following sign outside an Irish undertakers in 1813: 'Coffins, Made or Mended'.

∞

FAULKNERS Dublin Journal of 17 February 1761 records the following remarkable details: 'There is at present at New-Row in the Poddle, one Henry Golding, who has entered the 20th year of his age, and measures only 27 inches in height.'

⊷

IT is estimated that by 1860 some two thirds of the British Army was constituted by Irishmen or their descendants.

⊷

THE world's smallest crystal bowl was made by Jim Irish of Rathcilliheen, County Waterford in 2001. It was an amazing 8.55 mm (0.336 inches) wide, 4.6 mm (0.18 inches) tall, 2.1 mm (0.08 inches) thick and was made with over 208 cuts. It took eight hours for Mr Irish to complete the bowl over a two-week period, working it in 45 tiny segments.

⊷

A DUBLIN family who had buried their seven-year-old sister in a quiet country graveyard 30 years previously were overjoyed to discover that she was alive in 1961. No one knows exactly what happened. In the summer of 1931, Esther Kelly was stricken with diphtheria. Her parents rushed her to hospital, where doctors fought to save her life for six weeks. Then came good news. They were told they could take her home on 13 November. Next the family was told she had died. The stunned family called to the hospital. Esther's mother asked to see the body, but there was a mask over the child's face. Doctors told her that her face was disfigured and it would be better not to see it, so

126

the Kellys took the little coffin away and buried the child. Until she died in 1949, Mrs Kelly brought flowers to the grave every Sunday. Unbeknownst to her, Esther was alive and working as a domestic servant within five miles of her home. Esther's father died in 1961.

What really happened that crucial day 30 years previously? The record in the general registry of Ireland has an entry which says: 'Kelly, Esther, Died: Nov. 11 1931 in hospital of diphtheria (certified) 61 days illness.'

She is described as seven years, and a spinster and a labourer's child. It gives the name of the witness who was present at death and the address of the Kelly home. In the eyes of the law, Esther Kelly was dead. Hospital records show that Esther Kelly, aged seven, same address, had been treated for 61 days for diphtheria, and on 11 November 1931 was discharged as cured. The record also shows that the child was released to an orphanage. The records do not show that there was any other Esther Kelly.

From the first day in the orphanage, Esther insisted that she did not belong there and wanted to go home to her family. But nobody took any notice. She did not know where her home was or how to get there and eventually she gave up. She stayed in the orphanage for 10 years, then left to take up her job – ironically, within five miles of her home. When Esther emigrated to England years later, she needed a birth certificate for the first time. She wrote to the gardaí, who were able to discover the name of the parents of an Esther Kelly born in 1924. They were also able to locate her sister Elizabeth. Esther wrote to her and the result was a dramatic reunion at Dublin Airport.

Any doubts the Kellys had about this strange woman claiming to be their dead sister were laid to rest when one remembered that their sister had marks on her lips from stitches after she had cut her lip on a broken slate as a three-year-old. They fully accepted she was their sister when they saw that Esther had this mark. Though the story ended happily for the Kelly family, two mysteries remain to this day. How did this terrible mistake occur and who is the nameless child in Esther Kelly's grave?

❧

ROBERT Caldwell (1814–91) from Clady, County Armagh went to Madras in 1837 and lived his life in India as a missionary. He was also a scholar and wrote extensively on Indian history and languages. Most notably, he translated the Bible and the Book of Common Prayer into Tamil.

❧

THE world's largest free-standing Christmas card was made by students at University College, Dublin on 3 December 1990. It was as big as 4,500 regular-sized greeting cards put together. It was made from one piece of card with a surface area of 251 m² (2,700 square feet). The 30 m x 8.3 m (98 feet x 27 feet 2 inches) card was folded over. It then measured 15 m x 8.3 m (49 feet 2 inches x 27 feet 2 inches).

❧

A MONTY Python-esque scene saw sightseers flock to Dublin's Merrion Strand on 7 April 1978. A fire engine, a Land Rover and a tow truck were all stuck in wet sand. The unlikely chain of events began when the tow truck driver went to the aid of a motorist whose car had got trapped in the sand. The car was rescued easily enough, but the tow truck was left axle-deep in the sand. A Land Rover driver spotted the truck's plight and tried to help, but it too got stuck. Next came the fire engine and in minutes it had ended up like the other vehicles. A fire brigade Land Rover was called in and all the vehicles got back to firm ground before the tide came in.

❧

IRELAND'S greatest (but least-known) film star is veteran actor and stuntman Bronco McLaughlin from Ashford, County Wicklow. Since the 1960s, Bronco has worked in countless films and television series. Most likely you will not recall his name or remember his face, but he appeared in many of the big budget action films of the past five decades, including the Star Wars, James Bond and Indiana Jones film series. If you have ever watched *The Mission* (1985), Bronco is in the opening scenes tied to a wooden cross being swept down a raging waterfall.

❧

ON 3 March 1997, 27-year-old Alison Kennedy from Belfast was stabbed in the head while travelling by train from London to Guildford. It was a motiveless and random assault by a 17-year-old, who plunged a hunting dagger into her skull, burying it almost up to the hilt. Reports say the blade was over five inches long. It is not unusual that victims of such an attack are not immediately aware that they have been stabbed. Alison Kennedy was no different in this respect.

She first felt excruciating pain. 'I put my right hand up,' the brave woman later recalled. 'I knew there was something in my head.' During a two-and-a-half hour operation at the National Hospital for Neurology and Neurosurgery in London, the blade was removed. She was, of course, extremely unfortunate to have been a victim, but Alison was also incredibly lucky that the knife had not cut through important areas of her brain. It had missed the brain's blood supply by fractions of an inch and the area of the brain which controls vital functions. Had any damage occurred to the brain stem, she would have been completely paralysed.

The remarkable Belfast woman was discharged from the hospital after two weeks. Alison was left with some numbness in one arm and a degree of tunnel vision, but was reportedly otherwise physically unscathed. Her assailant was convicted of attempted murder.

⁂

IN January 1997, British taxpayers forked out £3,000 to an Irish artist to walk up and down inside a large wooden crate. Kevin Gray (aged 24) was awarded a council-funded art gallery grant to spend 10 weeks in his box after he won first prize in an exhibition at the Mostyn Gallery in Llandudno in Wales. For six hours each day he took seven steps forward and seven back inside the 20-foot-long crate. The judges described his bizarre exhibit as 'an extraordinary piece of work'.

Gray told reporters, 'My performance represents the idea of solitary confinement and the sensory deprivation torture inflicted on prisoners interrogated in Northern Ireland.' In keeping with the exhibit, the photograph accompanying the newspaper article showed Gray wearing a balaclava.

⁂

IF there were canine awards, Jock, an Alsatian, would have been decorated. The warmth from his large body helped keep two men alive through a numbing night of sleet and rain on an island in Lough Corrib, County Galway in mid-December 1984. It was Jock's first trip and his grateful owner, 23-year-old Donal Hegarty, vowed that it would not be his last. Donal and a friend, Gerry Mullins, had been rescued from a tiny island at Menlo, in the lower reaches of the Corrib. They had set out on Lough Corrib in a 15-foot boat early one Sunday morning to test a new engine.

Hours later, the engine failed and an oar broke as they attempted to row ashore. As darkness fell, the men knew there was little chance of rescue until the next day, so they tried to make themselves comfortable for the night. Donal had no coat and was freezing, but Jock climbed in between the two men and kept them warm. He also licked their faces as if to keep up their spirits. At 9:30 a.m., the two men were spotted by searchers.

One amazed garda officer said it had been a miracle that they had not died from exposure. 'There was no doubt that the warmth of the dog saved them,' he said. While Donal and Gerry were treated for exposure in Galway Regional Hospital, Jock was driven to the Hegarty home for a welcome meal. Afterwards he slumped down on the living room carpet in front of the fire and went to sleep, unfazed by all the attention.

∽

THE *Daily Mirror* of 26 February 1993 carried a strange report about a mystery from Dundalk, County Louth. For months the Bradley family had been suffering from headaches caused by a pungent smell which pervaded their house. Environmental officers lifted part of the floor in the sitting room and oil welled up. A trench dug outside the 90-year-old house soon filled up with crude oil too. It is generally thought that there is no oil in Ireland. Louth County Council said that the substance was not lubricating oil, diesel or petrol; scientists did not know what it was. An official report confirmed the presence of 'hydrocarbons of unknown origin'.

∽

ABRAHAM Abell (1773–1851) from Cork was a successful businessman and a generous philanthropist. He was a man of numerous interests and was heavily involved in many literary and learned societies throughout Ireland and Britain. It is thanks to him that the first collection of Ogham inscriptions ever made in Ireland now has a permanent home in University College, Cork.

Abell was endearingly eccentric. He would not have a fire in his room and kept himself warm in winter through vigorous exercise, such as skipping with a rope. On his birthday he liked to walk a mile for every year of his life. His last attempt was to walk from Cork to Youghal and back on his 58th birthday. Every morning, having sponged himself, Abell used to stand on an isolated stool and, by means of a silk handkerchief, communicate to his frame as much electricity as he thought sufficient for the day's use.

For a couple of weeks he slept between two skeletons to get over the fear of the supernatural which had been instilled in him from childhood. Normally he slept with his head resting on a pile of paper. The idiosyncratic Corkman often read late into the night. To help him stay awake, he always stood at his desk, sometimes on one foot. In a fit of depression, the poor man once burned his entire collection of books and musical scores. He regretted his actions shortly after and set about establishing a new collection.

≪

ON 29 August 1819, a terrible accident occurred at Carnglas, near Coleraine, County Antrim. A young servant boy was drawing water from a well when the bucket came off the rope and fell in. He was lowered on a rope and retrieved the bucket. As the boy was being hauled up, the sides of the well collapsed and caved in, burying the poor boy alive.

A crowd quickly gathered in an effort to retrieve the body (they thought it impossible that he was still alive). That day they worked hard and managed to clear out 16 feet. Next morning the work resumed, but became increasingly dangerous. At that level the earth was sandy and the sides constantly collapsed and had to be dug out again. It got so bad that all who were there refused to continue excavating the well in case they too were buried alive. They advised the young lad's master to fill in the well, but he would not stop the search, no matter what anyone said.

Two brave men, Archibald McMullin and Alexander Anderson, agreed to continue the dangerous task. Around three o'clock that afternoon, they heard a cry from beneath them. It startled them for a moment until they realised that it must have come from the boy, so they redoubled their efforts. As they dug deeper, they were encouraged by the sound of the boy speaking to them. Finally, at six o'clock, they found him, 26 feet from the surface (the well was 35 feet deep), surrounded by earth.

A large stone over the boy's head had supported the weight above, giving him a small air space and protecting him. The boy was tightly wedged in, but with a great deal of difficulty they managed to rescue him. The boy did not have any serious injuries, but his body was so swollen that his clothes had to be cut off. He made a full recovery.

∽

HENRY Dodwell (1641–1711) of Manor Dodwell, County Roscommon was one of the most learned men of his time, a famous scholar and theologian. Wherever he travelled, whether it was from Athlone to Dublin or from Holyhead to London, he went on foot with his pockets and bosom stuffed with books, reading every step of the way.

∽

IN his youth, Colonel Dudley Cosby (1670–1729) of Stradbally, County Laois was famous for his agility and athletic ability. He thought nothing of leaping over a fish pond 21 feet wide (on flat ground he could leap 24 feet). Cosby once had five horses lined up shoulder to shoulder. He put his hand on the first horse and vaulted into the saddle of the fifth horse. It is said that he could follow a pack of fleet hounds from morning until night and could keep up with them better than anyone on horseback. He was a brilliant all-round sportsman and was highly regarded as a fine hurler.

∽

THE mysterious disappearance of chickens near Ballydehob beach in County Cork was a cause of concern and puzzlement to the locals in August 1939. One day, a cat was spotted moving about among the fowl, when a large seagull swooped down and seized a chicken in its beak. The cat attacked the bird, which released the chicken and grabbed the cat, soaring aloft with her. About 15 feet from the ground, the seagull let the cat drop. The cat lived up to its reputation of having nine lives.

§

THE Dublin Penny Journal of 1833 recounts a strange story of canine intelligence and ability, which is said to have occurred in Belfast around 1810. An unnamed Belfast family had a one-year-old gun dog called Neptune, which they gave away to some friends, the Scott family, who lived three-quarters of a mile away. Although Neptune settled in well with his new owners, he occasionally visited his original owners. One day the Scotts made a present of nine young ducks to Neptune's previous owners.

The next morning, Mrs Scott was astonished to see them back safe and sound at her kitchen door. No one had any idea how they had found their way there. They were not fully grown and were unable to fly. She returned the ducks to their new owners and thought that would be the end of the matter. The next morning, Mrs Scott could not believe her eyes. They were back again! Two of the ducks were killed for dinner and Mrs Scott personally delivered the other seven back to their new owners.

Every now and again the ducks would return to the Scotts, who would return them to their new home. Just how these young ducks made their way through three close-barred gates and travelled a mile in the short space of a night remained a mystery for several months until a gentleman passing by the Scotts spotted Neptune and recognised him as the same dog he had met on the road several months before, just before sunrise, driving ducks, and carrying in his mouth a lame one which was unable to travel.

❧

IN the early hours of 3 April 2001, alarms went off at Leinster House in Dublin (home of the Dáil and Seanad). Gardaí chased a fox through the corridors, but it managed to escape through an open window.

❧

CENTENARIAN huntsman Daniel O'Callaghan (1763–1874) from Mallow, County Cork rode to hounds when he was 103 years of age. He died eight years later.

❧

IN the market square of Comber, County Down stands a monument to Major-General Rollo Gillespie (1766–1814), one of the most remarkable adventurers Ireland has produced. At the age of 17, Gillespie joined the British army. At 20 he fell in love and eloped with his sweetheart. A few weeks after his marriage, he fought a duel over a handkerchief with the brother of Sir Jonah Barrington, whom he killed. At 26 he went to Jamaica. On the voyage out, he was shipwrecked and managed to escape in an open boat in heavy seas. In Jamaica he saw a great deal of fighting and suffered several wounds. One night, returning to his quarters, he was attacked by eight brigands. Gillespie killed six with his sword and the other two fled for their lives. Later, in India, with only 1,500 men, he captured a fort defended by 100 guns and 30,000 sepoys. Gillespie's death was romantic. He fell, shot through the heart, crying, 'One more shot for the honour of Down.'

❧

IN 1821, Langham, an Irish footman in the service of Lord Berkeley, made a round trip of 148 miles in less than 42 hours on foot in order to pick up medicine from a London doctor for the peer's sick wife. As a reward, Lady Berkeley gave him a new suit of clothes. This remarkable feat is recorded in the *Berkeley Manuscripts* (1821).

❧

JANE Williams of Dublin currently has a collection of over 1,000 elephant statues or ornaments. She started her collection at the age of 10, purchasing a tiny jade elephant from a shop on Grafton Street for £10 after saving all her pocket money for three years to buy it. Jane first saw the elephant at an auction at Birr Castle, County Offaly three years before, but did not pay much attention to it at the time. She could have bought it for £1 then. Jane picked up many of her ornaments on her travels in Africa, India and the Far East, but one her most interesting elephants is an oriental papier-mâché one that once belonged to Hilton Edwards, the theatre manager, actor and director.

❧

ON 1 September 2003, Gertie Clarke was at home in Hill Street, Ballina, County Mayo. At 11:20 a.m. she heard a loud bang, went outside and discovered that a salmon weighing 4½ lb (2 kg) had smashed into her roof, breaking a slate, before getting lodged. Pieces of the fish were splattered on the roof and on the ground below. It is believed that the fish had been dropped from a considerable height by an osprey after catching the salmon in the nearby River Moy.

~§

A REMARKABLE recovery was reported by doctors of the Jervis Street Hospital in Dublin on 27 August 1917. Six months previously Private Stephen Conroy of the Leinster Regiment was wounded in action fighting the Germans in France during World War I. The fifty-four-year-old was injured and knocked unconscious for five days by an exploding shell. When Conroy came to, he had lost his speech and hearing. The father of six was sent to a depot for the wounded in Birr, County Offaly to recover. In mid-August he was moved to Jervis Street Hospital to be treated by a throat and ear specialist. Conroy's condition remained unchanged there. To his doctor's surprise, Conroy's speech and hearing returned overnight in late August. Conroy explained that at 2 a.m. that morning he dreamed he saw the figure of a woman standing at his bedside commanding him to pray. He was so startled that involuntarily he shouted and then discovered he had regained his speech and hearing.

~§

IT is possible to fill many pages with accounts of remarkable Irish centenarians. However, as one person pointed out to me, the Irish are great storytellers and prone to exaggeration. The longest-lived Irish person whose birth and death can be authenticated is Annie Scott, who lived for 113 years and 37 days. She was born in Dungannon,

County Tyrone on 15 March 1883 and moved to Ballybay, County Monaghan when she married in 1915. Annie moved to Scotland in 1971 to live with her son Tom. This remarkable woman died on 21 April 1996 at the Church of Scotland home in Reay, near Thurso, Caithness, where she had lived since 1972. A strict Presbyterian who never touched alcohol or tobacco, she remained sprightly to the end, but went blind in her last few months. She never took any medicine, not even an aspirin.

The runner-up in this category of record is the Honourable Katherine Plunket from County Louth, who lived for 111 years and 342 days. She was born on 22 November 1820 and passed away peacefully at her home on 14 October 1932. She remembered sitting on the writer Sir Walter Scott's knee at the age of five and had an active mind until the end. Katherine had a keen interest in current affairs and enjoyed having the daily papers read to her every day. Until she was 100, she was driven to church every Sunday in a carriage drawn by four white horses.

∽

ECCENTRIC, physically healthy Lord Emly of Tervoe, County Limerick, spent the last 15 years of his life (1879–94) in a four-poster bed, with the curtains drawn.

∽

A EWE belonging to the Eakin family of Ballymoile, Moneymore, County Derry gave birth to two lambs on 3 April 1911. She gave birth to two more lambs on 23 April. They were all born alive and thrived.

∽

IN October 2001, an otherwise normal Atlantic brown crab with a double claw was caught in the Irish Sea by fishermen from County Down. Coghan Mac Guibhir from Carrick, County Donegal was given the claw by his sister-in-law, who worked at a fish-processing factory at Errigal. His father, a fisherman for nearly 50 years, had never seen anything like it.

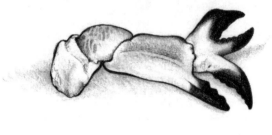

⤪

A CROSS-country golf competition was organised as part of Ireland's three-week national festival of An Tostal in 1953. Some 150 golfers played from the first tee at Kildare Town Club with the aim of holing out on the 18th green of the Curragh course, five miles away. Among the natural hazards between the two golf courses were the main Dublin to Cork railway line and road, the Curragh Racecourse, a maze of army tank tracks and about 150 telephone posts. The winner was Irish International champion Joe Carr with a score of 52.

⤪

THE best man mistakenly married the bride at a wedding at Killeter Presbyterian Church in County Tyrone in November 1937. Twenty-one-year-old Albert Muldoon was best man for his good friend Christopher Craig. He brought the bridal pair to the church in his car and took the bride in on his arm, leaving her at the front of altar. He remained standing beside her. Nobody asked who he was as he stood between the bride and bridegroom.

The clergyman, Reverend Duncan, naturally addressed his questions to Albert, never having seen the couple before. He had agreed to marry the couple on behalf of the minister at the neighbouring Second Castlederg Presbyterian Church. 'When it came to the part where the clergyman asked me a question, mentioning "Christopher Craig", I knew somebody had made a mistake,' Albert later told reporters. 'When he asked me a second time, I answered him. I think we all knew a mistake had been made, but nobody understood what should be done.

'After the service, as he was getting ready for us to sign the register, Rev. W. Duncan looked at me and said: "Have you ever been married before?" I knew then for certain that he was taking me for the bridegroom and I replied: "No doubt you are making a mistake, your reverence." "Who are you then?" Rev. Duncan said and I replied, "I'm Muldoon, the driver. I'm the best man." The clergyman asked us why this had not been mentioned before and we then went through the whole ceremony again, making sure that there were no mistakes.

Albert Muldoon explained to reporters that he was not familiar with the Presbyterian form of marriage, being a member of the Church of Ireland. No harm was done because a wedding is not legal until the register has been signed.

❦

THE Garden Cottage at Killedan House, County Roscommon was built with a chimney at each corner of the dwelling.

∽

IN the *Dublin Quarterly Journal of Medical Sciences* (vol. XV), Dr Montgomery describes conjoined twin sisters born in Boyle, County Roscommon on 24 July 1827. They had two heads, two chests with arms complete, two abdominal and pelvic cavities united end to end and four legs, placed two on either side. The twins had only one anus, which was situated between the thighs on one side. One was dark-haired and was baptised Mary, while the other was a blonde and was named Catherine. These twins felt and acted independently of each other. They each in succession sucked from the breast or took milk from the spoon, and used their limbs vigorously. One vomited without affecting the other, but the faeces were discharged through a common opening. They died two days later.

∽

ONLY one diamond has ever been discovered in Ireland, but its origins are still a mystery. It was found in the early 19th century in the Colebrook River, near Enniskillen, County Fermanagh, by a girl who later gave it to the local landowners, the Brookeborough family. No one knows how the diamond came to be found in the river. The Brookeborough family was thought to have known some diamond importers at the time, so it may not even be of Irish origin. Tests could prove where the precious gem originated, but the family was never interested in having it analysed.

∽

THE first parachute jump in Ireland took place on 14 September 1889 at Clonturk Park, Drumcondra, Dublin. The National Library of Ireland has a poster advertising the event and displaying a handsome portrait of the parachutist Percival Spenser, who had already jumped over the main cities of India. A huge, uncontrollable crowd assembled to witness the 'madman' jumping from a balloon. They were not disappointed by what they saw. At 6:30 p.m. Spencer ascended to 2,500 feet in his balloon, checked his parachute and jumped, landing only 400 yards from where he had started.

An ingenious device fitted to the balloon ensured that it emptied itself of gas immediately after Spenser had jumped. The balloon was ballasted so that it turned over after he had leaped out and the gas quickly escaped from the open neck. Parachutes were not a new concept to Ireland. As early as 21 July 1817, a Miss Thompson had dropped a tortoise attached to a parachute from a balloon over Dublin.

∽

THESE two eggs (joined together by a neck about half an inch wide) were laid by a hen owned by John O'Donnell, Oxford Farm, Kiltimagh, County Mayo.

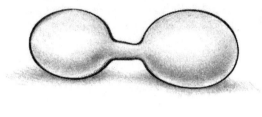

∽

ANNIE Allan from Cookstown, County Tyrone emigrated to New York in 1856 when she was 14 years old. By the age of 18 she weighed more than 300 pounds. Two years later, she was hired as a sideshow attraction by a canny promoter and went on tour as The Fat Girl. In 1884 she married Charles Price on stage before a paying audience at the New York Museum. They were an unlikely couple, hence the attraction of public interest.

At her peak Annie weighed 525 pounds and Charles was a tall, well-built albino, who was known as the Great Albino King. Annie's weight plummeted (for her) down to 400 pounds during the course of an unspecified illness in 1889. She never recovered and died with Charles by her side. She lay in state in an ice box for three days so that the curious (paying) onlookers could take one last look at one of America's most famous attractions. In order to prevent a mob from gathering at her funeral, Annie was buried in Evergreens Cemetery well after midnight.

∽

CHEESE-and-onion-flavoured crisps were invented by Dublin entrepreneur Joseph Murphy in 1954. Murphy founded Tayto crisps earlier that year after being dissatisfied with the quality of other crisps on the market. Spotting a gap in the market for decent crisps, he travelled to England to learn how they were made and bought the equipment necessary to start his own crisp company. On 26 March 1954 the first Tayto potato crisps were cooked and packed in bags in a tiny premises in O'Rahilly's Parade off Dublin's Moore Street. From small beginnings, the business flourished and is now a thriving concern that exports its products all around the world.

Tayto is now owned by another entrepreneur, Meath man Raymond Coyle. He has never been afraid to take risks and is most famous as being the first buffalo (more properly called American bison) farmer in Ireland. He imported a herd from Yellowstone National Park in the United States.

∽

IN March 1911, a small County Mayo farmer bought a cow which fell ill and died two weeks later. A local butcher performed a post-mortem examination and discovered several strange objects in the unfortunate animal's stomach. Inside a leather clasp purse he found four sovereigns, one half-sovereign, a half-crown, threepence in coppers and a railway ticket to Mullingar. On further examination, a brass doorknob, three breech-loading cartridges and a quantity of black glass (possibly from porter bottles) were discovered. This broken glass was the likely cause of the animal's demise.

∽

IN January 1960, a rat was spotted crossing the River Blackwater near Mallow, County Cork perched on a swan's back. On another occasion Dublin journalist Joseph Mac-Cullough saw the same thing on the Tolka River at the rear of Richmond Road, Drumcondra, Dublin.

❧

EIGHTY-five-year-old Dr Dermot Lyne of Ardgroom, Berehaven, County Cork died in the early half of the 18th century. His house was built to a very unusual design. Every window had another opposite it, none of which was ever glazed or shuttered. They were left open permanently, even in stormy weather. Dr Lyne's bedroom had two open windows on each side of his bed. Strangely, for 50 years nobody had died in the house, even though Lyne had a large family. After his death, the first thing his heir did was to have glass put in all the windows.

❧

THE Comeragh Mountains of County Waterford were home to two remarkable hermits in the early decades of the 20th century. The more famous of these colourful gentlemen was Jim Fitzgerald (1891–1959) from Ballymacarby. He returned home from World War I a shell-shocked and broken man. The horrors of what he had witnessed fighting against the Turks at Gallipoli remained with him for all of his days, but Jim found peace in the mountains, where he lived in a cave for the rest of his life. Occasionally he left his retreat to collect his war pension and buy supplies. Jim was a well-liked figure and was widely known in Ireland and abroad because of his rare interviews with journalists. After many decades of being exposed to the elements, the hermit developed pneumonia and died in hospital.

The lesser-known hermit of the Comeraghs must at least have been a passing acquaintance of Fitzgerald. The only mention of this eccentric Waterford man I can find is in the *Waterford Star* of 1 August 1930. Mike Curran had been a fireman on the Waterford and Limerick Railway, a soldier in the British army (including five years' service in India) and had lived in England for a decade before returning to Waterford to live in little more than a burrow in the mountainside. Asked if he was happy there, Mike replied, 'Well begor, sir, I wouldn't change it for Buckingham Palace.' He made a living fishing and working on farms in the neighbourhood.

࿇

MEATH-born Margaret Ball (1514–84) was the wife of a mayor of Dublin, mother of two mayors of Dublin and grandmother of two mayors of Dublin. In 1580 her son Walter was elected mayor. Because she refused to renounce her Catholic faith and swear loyalty to Queen Elizabeth I, Walter had his 65-year-old mother arrested and jailed. The rest of the Ball family were powerless to do anything and she died in prison fours years later. Margaret would have been freed if she had done what her son had asked. Despite the cruel treatment she had endured, she left all her property to Walter. The title of Lord Mayor of Dublin did not come into use until 1665.

࿇

THE fastest ever walk over the 644 km (400 miles, 350 yards) from Malin Head, County Donegal to Mizen

Head, County Cork is 5 days, 22 hours and 30 minutes, by John 'Paddy' Dowling between 18 and 24 March 1982.

≪

THE Dublin Penny Journal of 1832 describes an instance of sleepwalking that nearly led to disaster. Edward Harding was a student at Trinity College, Dublin. He occupied an attic in the left wing of the university and occasionally sleepwalked on the roof at night. One night he gave shelter to a relation who had been locked out of his own residence. They shared Harding's bed and settled down for the night. They had not been in bed more than two hours when his relative saw Harding get up, dress, strike a light and sit down apparently to study. This did not surprise his relation, who thought Harding was preparing for approaching exams.

A few minutes later, he watched Harding open a window and climb out onto the roof. Remembering that Harding sometimes sleepwalked, his relative cautiously pursued him. The day was just dawning and he could see Harding walking along a parapet. Afraid for Harding's life, his relative crawled along the roof gutter until he reached Harding, who now was standing at the extreme end of the building and seemed to be contemplating the ground far below.

He grabbed Harding's arm and pulled him into the gutter, holding him there by force, until Harding awoke and became aware of their perilous situation. He never sleepwalked again, although he used to get out of bed at night and mope about for a minute or two. He would quickly awake terrified, then calm down and go back to bed and sleep the rest of the night undisturbed.

≪

LILLIAN Bland (1878–1971) from Tobarcooran House, Carnmoney, near Belfast, was the first woman in the world to design, build and fly an airplane. Inspired by Louis Blériot's cross-Channel flight in 1909, she decided to build her own plane. In 1910 her biplane, the *Mayfly*, took off from Carnmoney Hill and flew for a quarter of a mile.

৯

IN the 1860s, Lord Wallscourt of Ardfry Castle, County Galway liked to roam naked through his house. His wife made him wear a cowbell to warn maids of his approach.

৯

DURING World War I, Cobh, County Cork – then called Queenstown – with its magnificent harbour, was the naval base for the American navy while it operated in European waters. Consequently, the town was crowded with sailors on 'shore leave'. Cork city itself was strictly out of bounds for the sailors, so Cobh had to entertain the many thousands of servicemen who came ashore. The one tourist attraction in the area was the world-famous Blarney Castle. It was 21 miles from Cobh – too long a journey for a horse to accomplish in an afternoon – so the enterprising jarveys of Cobh devised a cunning ruse to placate the many sailors who wanted to kiss the famous Blarney Stone.

About two miles from Cobh lay Belvelly Castle, an old ruin that was fairly similar to Blarney Castle, close enough anyway to deceive any naïve overseas tourist. The sailors were brought out in droves by the canny jarveys to see the castle and kiss the 'Blarney Stone'! When asked once by a fellow Irishman to point out which impostor stone was being paraded as the 'Blarney', one jarvey replied, 'Yerra, any one at all, sir, as long as t'was a bit hard to git at. Most of them stones round the top have had their share. Shure, there's bits of chewing-gum stuck all over them!'

❦

A SMALL black and white dog had a miraculous survival on a wintry night in November 2006. It travelled all the way from Coleraine to Belfast, a distance of around 100 km (60 miles), wedged in the grille of a Peugeot 306 and clinging on for its life. The driver thought he had hit something on the dual carriageway outside Coleraine after hearing a thud, but saw nothing in his rear view mirror and continued, unaware that he had picked up a passenger. It was only when he got out at the Odyssey Arena in Belfast that he heard a barking sound coming from the front bonnet. After such an ordeal, the dog was understandably grumpy, and he was nicknamed Father Jack, after the cantankerous priest in the television sitcom *Father Ted*. Although the dog was obviously distressed by the ordeal, he escaped with only minor injuries and amazingly had no broken bones. When he was brought to the Eastwood Veterinary Hospital in east Belfast, the dog was treated for hypothermia, but quickly recovered. He was not wearing a collar, but was reunited with his owner, Robert Campbell, after a television appeal. Sadly, however, on 13 December (three weeks after his death-defying ride), 12-year-old 'Father Jack' was run over and killed by a grocery van in his own backyard.

❦

AN Irish attempt to set a new world record for the biggest beard of bees ended in disaster on 25 June 2005, with many onlookers getting stung in Cahir, County Tipperary. Veteran beekeeper Philip McCabe managed to attract 200,000 bees (about 60 lb) to congregate on his body at once – but was 150,000 bees short of the world record (87½ lb) set in America in 1988. A large crowd of spectators gathered to watch him attempt to set a new bizarre record to raise money for charity. Neither McCabe nor any of the crowd were stung until he jumped off the weighing scales after deciding to end his attempt.

∽

A COUNTY Galway member of Dáil Éireann, Brídget Hogan, made Irish political history in April 1958 when she married Deputy Michael O'Higgins from County Kildare. It was the first ever wedding between Dáil deputies, and Mr and Mrs O'Higgins were the first husband and wife team to sit in the Irish legislative assembly. In July 2005, Olwyn Enright from County Offaly married Senator Joe McHugh from County Donegal. He was elected to the Dáil in 2007, making them the second married couple to be elected to sit in the same Dáil.

∽

IT was not in India, but on Donnybrook Road in Dublin that Arthur Wellesley (later Duke of Wellington) won his first victory. On 17 September 1789, the 20-year-old Lieutenant Wellesley bet famous Wicklow gambler Thomas 'Buck' Whaley that he could walk a specified distance in a given time for a wager of 150 guineas.

The starting point was a marker known as the 'Five Mile Stone', which stuck out from the boundary wall of Cabinteely House beyond Cornelscourt village. From that point, the future commander-in-chief of the British army and victor of Waterloo set out on foot for Dublin on 18 September, accompanied by several gentlemen on horseback. At times the horsemen had to put their mounts into a smart trot to keep up with him. Fifty-five minutes later, the determined lieutenant had travelled six miles of rough 18th-century road and reached the junction of Leeson Street and Adelaide Road to win his bet and make his first mark on history.

❧

THOMAS Lighton from Strabane, County Tyrone was a failed shopkeeper who went out to India as a soldier to support his wife and child back home. He had a talent for languages and was frequently called upon by his superiors to act as an interpreter. Lighton was a member of the garrison at Bednore, under General Matthews, when the fortress was taken by Tippo Sultan of Mysore in 1783.

Under orders, Lighton managed to escape. He had been entrusted to deliver the general's valuables to his wife in London. After many adventures, Lighton succeeded in reaching England, where he handed over the valuables and a poignant last letter from Matthews (who knew he would be killed). As a reward for the Irishman's honesty, the general's widow gave him the enormous sum of £20,000. Lighton and his family later settled in Dublin. The honest Strabane man established a bank and earned himself a baronetcy and lived out the rest of his life at Merville House, Dundrum. Upon his death in 1805, he was buried in Taney Church of Ireland Graveyard, Dundrum. His former home is now part of University College, Dublin.

∽

THIRTY-THREE-year-old Padraig Marrey from Ballinrobe, County Mayo set a new record for cycling the length of Ireland on 27 August 2006. He set off from Mizen Head, County Cork at 5 a.m. and arrived at Fair Head, County Antrim 17 hours, 38 minutes and 28 seconds later, beating the previous record by almost an hour.

∽

A 45-KM fence built to contain Glenveagh National Park's red deer herd in County Donegal is reputedly Ireland's longest.

∽

IN his will, Sir Robert Holmes (1622–92) from Mallow, County Cork made ample provision for his illegitimate daughter, Mary Holmes, and left the bulk of his fortune to his nephew Henry Holmes from Kilmallock, County Limerick on condition that he marry Mary inside 18 months. Sir Robert's wishes were carried out and the cousins married, keeping the family fortune intact.

∽

THE spectacular Mourne Wall is Ireland's longest wall. It was built around the Mourne Mountains in County Down, Northern Ireland between 1904 and 1922 by the Belfast Water Commissioners, to enclose the water catchment in the Mournes and to keep out animals. The dry stone wall was built with local granite and is about

2.5 metres high and 1 metre thick. It is 35 km (22 miles) long and passes over 15 mountains.

≼

IN 1962, Susie, a collie dog owned by Dennis Curtin of Brosna, near Tralee in County Kerry, raised two piglets alongside her own puppy. Thinking that she was their mother, the piglets followed her everywhere. A remarkable photograph of Susie and her piglets and puppy appeared in a local paper at the time.

≼

SHORTLY after midnight on 16 May 1950, a prominent Limerick citizen on his way home looked up after hearing a strange noise in the sky. He was astonished to see a ball of fire passing overheard at a great height. 'The ball of fire was a glowing mass of red flame,' he later told a reporter from *The Irish Times*. 'It was taking an east–west direction a little to the south of Rineanna. Its altitude was greater than any plane I have ever seen.' It had a circular motion and, though it did not make any mechanical noise, it caused considerable air disturbance, creating a sort of vacuum as it passed. The Limerick man told his tale because he wondered if anyone else had witnessed this phenomenon.

※

DECLAN O'Rourke from County Wicklow lost his wedding ring while scuba-diving off Australia on his honeymoon in April 2003. He never expected to see it again, but months later Paul Walker from Manchester was scuba-diving in the same spot and found the ring stuck in a coral reef. A jeweller told him it was Irish and the couple's names and wedding date were engraved inside, so Paul decided to trace them. He went on 2FM's *Gerry Ryan Show* in July 2004 and appealed to listeners to help him trace the ring's owners. Paul Walker was delighted when the astonished couple got in touch and he was able to return the ring in person.